B29: the superfortress

BB

B29:

Carl Berger

the superfortress

Editor-in-Chief: Barrie Pitt
Art Director: Peter Dunbar
Military Consultant: Sir Basil Liddell Hart
Picture Editor: Bobby Hunt
Editor: David Mason
Design: Sarah Kingham
Special Drawings: John Batchelor
Cartographer: Richard Natkiel
Photographic Research: Nan Shuttleworth

Photographs for this book were especially selected from the following Archives:
from left to right page 2–3 Boeing Co; 6–7 William Green; 6–9 US National Archives; 10–13 US Air Force; 14–15 William
Green/US Air Force; 16 Boeing Co; 17–19 William Green; 20 US Air Force; 21–23 William Green; 26–27 US Air Force; 28
Boeing Co; 28–29 US Air Force; 30–31 William Green; 32–35 Boeing Co; 36–39 Imperial War Museum; 40–42 US Army;
43 US Air Force; 44 US National Archives/IWM/US National Archives; 46–47 US Air Force; 49 Boeing Co; 51 William Green;
50–51 William Green; 52 US National Archives; 52 William Green; 54 IWM; 56–57 US Air Force; 56 US Air Force; 58–61 William
Green; 62–63 Hideya Ando; 63–66 US Air Force; 68 US Army; 70–71 US Air Force; 72 Keystone; 73 IWM/US Air Force;
73–86 US Air Force; 87 Keystone; 88–91 William Green; 91–93 US Air Force; 95 US Army; 96–116 US Air Force; 118 Keystone;
121–124 US Air Force; 130–131 Keystone; 130 Keystone; 132 US Air Force/IWM; 133–135 US Air Force; 136–137 IWM; 138
William Green/William Green/US Army; 140–147 US Air Force; 148 US National Archives; 150–154 US Air Force;
157 Australian War Memorial; 158 William Green/William Green/Boeing Co

Copyright © 1970 by Carl Berger

ISBN 0-345-24994-1-250

Manufactured in the United States of America

First Edition: October 1970
Fourth Printing: April 1977

Contents

Origins

The B-29 strategic bomber, the most powerful, most destructive weapon of the Second World War, had antecedents in the Great War of 1914-1918. During that first world conflict, Germany fielded history's first strategic bombing force, as Lieutenant-Colonel Raymond H Fredette has noted so perceptively in *The First Battle of Britain*. From Belgian bases, German pilots attacked British territory with several types of aircraft including the Giant bomber, which had a wing span only three feet shorter than the B-29. Beginning with their first strike on 19th-20th January 1915, German Zeppelins and Gotha and Giant bombers dropped 270 tons

Above: The Gotha G III of 1916, the immediate forerunner of the G IV which took over the strategic bombing of England in the summer of 1917. *Below:* The Zeppelin L48, destroyed while leading five airships in an attack on London on the night of 16th-17th June, 1917

of explosive on London and other parts of England, killing more than 1,400 people. The British reaction was severe and led, among other things, to formation of a separate Air Ministry and the Royal Air Force and creation of an Independent Air Force in France in June 1918 under Major-General Hugh Trenchard. Trenchard's primary mission was to pay the Germans back in kind. Flying DeHavilland and Handley Page aircraft, the Independent Air Force during the last months of the war attacked German industrial centers at Mannheim, Karlsruhe, Frankfurt, Coblenz, and Stuttgart. In all, they dropped 540 tons of bombs on Germany and killed approximately 700 persons. Trenchard was preparing to raid Berlin when the war ended.

In creating an independent air arm, the British government implemented recommendations submitted by a committee headed by General Jan Christiaan Smuts, the famed South African leader. In his report, he visualized the new aerial weapon as being possibly used 'as an independent means of war operations', pointing out that, unlike artillery, an air fleet 'can conduct extensive operations far from, and independently of, both Army and Navy. As far as at present can be foreseen, there is absolutely no limit to the scale of its future independent use. And the day may not be far off when aerial operations, with their devastation of enemy lands and destruction of industrial and populous centres on a vast scale, may become

the principal operations of war, to which the older forms of military and naval operations may become secondary and subordinate'.

This view, not surprisingly, found little support – on both sides of the Atlantic – among the generals and admirals. They challenged both the idea of independent air operations and the theory that the airplane would ever subordinate armies and navies. In America, one of the true believers in air power, Brigadier-General William 'Billy' Mitchell – who had served as a successful air commander on the Western Front – captured world headlines in 1921 when his squadrons sank a number of captured German warships during bombing tests in Chesapeake Bay. Mitchell

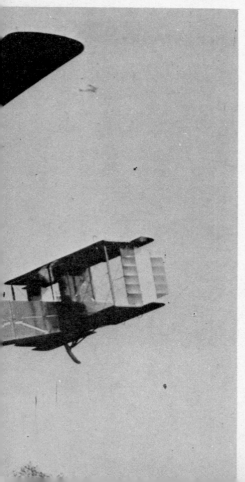

thought the British example well worth emulating and he agitated for an independent US air force, despite the disapproval of his superiors including General John J Pershing, Army Chief of Staff. Pershing made his views clear in his final report to the Secretary of War on 13th September 1924, the day before his retirement. The American Air Service, he said, constituted 'an essential aid to the armies in the field' as an auxiliary arm, whose best results were produced 'by the closest cooperation with the ground troops'.

Pershing scorned the claims of the airmen. Their tales 'of havoc done to enemy cities and installations' in the war had proved false, he said, ground inspections having found the damage almost 'negligible'. In a future war, he conceded, there would be 'somewhat greater damage' from aerial bombardment, but armies 'must still fight our battles – and to win must overcome the opposing forces' on the ground. As for Mitchell's celebrated demonstration over Chesapeake Bay, Pershing argued that 'improvements in the accuracy of antiaircraft artillery appear to be keeping pace with improvements in aviation'.

Despite this criticism, Mitchell could not refrain from publicizing his views. Even following his dismissal from his job in Washington as Assistant Chief of the Air Service and exile to San Antonio, Texas, he refused to be silenced. In September 1925, when the Navy dirigible *Shenandoah* cracked up and killed its commander and thirteen other men, Mitchell issued a statement to the press accusing the Navy and Army high commands of 'incompetency, criminal negligence, and almost treasonable administration of our national defense.' Brought before a court-martial in Washington, he was found

Handley Page 0/400, first British heavy bomber to be built in really large numbers. A US built Liberty-engined 0/400 is seen here on the left

Lieutenant Donald L Putt who survived the crash of the B299, prototype B-17, in which he was co-pilot, in 1935

guilty of insubordination by a panel of Army generals who recommended he be suspended 'from rank, command, and duty, with forfeiture of all pay and allowances, for five years.' Shortly after President Calvin Coolidge approved the sentence in January 1926, Mitchell resigned his Army commission to take his case for air power to the American people.

In the post-Mitchell era of the late 1920s, the Air Service was reorganized as the Army Air Corps but with little real change in its status. His followers, however, found some comfort in the continuing advances in aeronautical technology. For the Air Corps, a noteworthy event was the construction, beginning in 1930, of the twin-engine B-9, the world's first all-metal bomber. Like the B-29, it was a product of the Boeing Aircraft Company of Seattle, Washington. After flying the first experimental model in April 1931, Boeing delivered the plane to Wright Field, Dayton, Ohio – the Air Corps' development and test center. Impressed by its performance – it achieved a top speed of 188mph at 6,000 feet – the Army purchased the prototype and ordered six more.

The B-9, however, was quickly superseded by two other bombers built by the Martin Company, Denver, Colorado. One was the B-10, an all-metal prototype with retractable gear. During tests at Wright Field in July 1932, the aircraft flew at a top speed of 197mph at 6,000 feet. After new engines were installed, in October 1932 it flew at 207mph at 21,000 feet. Impressed by this superior performance, the Air Corps on 17th January 1934 ordered forty-eight production B-10s at a cost of $2,440,000. Additional improvements subsequently introduced into the aircraft increased its maximum speed to 213mph and its service ceiling to 24,200 feet. The plane was able to carry a maximum bomb load of about 2,200 pounds. The second Martin bomber, the B-12, did not show any significantly greater performance and the Air Corps decided to purchase the B-10 in substantial numbers.

Thus, of 115 planes ordered in fiscal year 1934, 91 were B-10B's. These Martin bombers were still being operated by Army squadrons when the Japanese struck Pearl Harbor. In 1934 one of Billy Mitchell's disciples, Lieutenant-Colonel Henry H 'Hap' Arnold, led a flight of ten B-10 bombers to Alaska in a test of the Air Corps, ability to reinforce US possessions by air. On their return from the 8,200 mile round trip, the planes flew nonstop over the ocean from Juneau, Alaska, to Seattle. Also, in February 1938, B-10's of the Chinese Air Force 'raided' Nagasaki, Japan, dropping leaflets telling the people that the 'China Incident' was far from closed.

Looking beyond the B-10, the Air Corps early in 1934 wrote a new specification for an aircraft which could carry 4,400 pounds of bombs, double that of the B-10. A design submitted by Douglas Aircraft, Santa Monica, California, was selected, designated the B-18, and the firm awarded a contract for 133 bombers in January 1936. The Air Corps ordered another batch the following year and, by 1940, most of the Air Corps' bomber squadrons were equipped with the twin-engine B-18s or B-18As These twin-engine bombers had a top speed of 217mph.

Long before the B-18s became operational, engineering officers at Wright Field drew up plans for an even more advanced long-range bomber. Their purpose was to implement a January 1933 War Department mission statement which authorized the Air Corps – previously limited to the land-based air defense of the coasts of the United States and its overseas possessions – to undertake long-range reconnaissance and operations 'to the limits of the radius of action of the airplanes.' To extend those limits, the Air Corps proposed a development known as 'Project A,' an aircraft with a 5,000 mile range which could carry a 2,000 pound bomb load. The Army approved the project after Air Corps officials pointed out that such an aircraft could help protect both Hawaii and Alaska. A single-prototype contract was awarded to Boeing, which began work in the summer of 1934. When completed, this four-engine experimental bomber – designated the XB-15 – had a wing span of 149 feet and a fuselage 87 feet 7 inches long. As it turned out, the bomber's gross weight of 92,000 pounds proved too heavy for the engines then available. The XB-15's top speed came to only 190mph.

While it was being assembled, Wright Field engineers wrote a specification for a more modest, 2,000 mile range bomber, which could carry a ton of bombs at speeds of 250mph. Boeing also received the contract for this plane, designated the XB-17, which flew for the first time on 28th July 1935. Powered by four Pratt & Whitney engines, the bomber was notable for its five gun emplacements, which immediately earned it the sobriquet, 'Flying Fortress.' In its preliminary trials, the XB-17 surpassed all the airmen's specifications for speed, climb, range, and load carrying capability. On 30th October

Brigadier-General William 'Billy' Mitchell demonstrated the bomber's potency in July 1921 when a few Martin NBS-Is sank the captured battleship *Ostfriesland*

1935, however, a fatal accident occurred. During takeoff on another test run, the prototype crashed at Wright Field, killing Boeing's test pilot, Leslie Tower, and Major Ployer P Hill of the Air Corps. Among those who survived was a young test pilot and engineer, Lieutenant Donald L Putt, who would later play an important role in the development of the B-29.

The loss of the prototype was a severe blow to the Air Corps. Reacting to the tragedy, the Army General Staff reduced the production order for the bomber from sixty-five to thirteen planes. In time, the bugs were worked out of the Flying Fortress and it was the only modern bomber in the US inventory when the Second World War began. The aeronautical technology that led to the B-17 and its predecessors later contributed substantially to the development of the B-29.

While various improvements were being made in long-range bombers, many people in Europe and America had become increasingly concerned about the role military aircraft might play in future wars. As early as 1923

the Hague Convention of Jurists attempted to establish some guidelines in this sensitive area by declaring that bombardment from the air 'is legitimate only when directed at a military objective ...' There were others who believed that the safety of their countries could only be assured by the total abolition of military aircraft. The British, who had suffered under air attack during the war, proved unwilling, however, to support complete air disarmament. In a draft treaty submitted to the disarmament conference in Geneva on 19th March 1933, they suggested that all countries 'accept the complete abolition of bombing from the air (except for police purposes in certain outlying regions).' This reservation followed the discovery of how useful military aircraft were in policing the British Empire.

The exception disturbed the new President of the United States, Franklin D Roosevelt, who sent word to the American delegation at Geneva that their ultimate goal 'must be to forbid any and all use of aircraft in land and sea war.' On 16th May 1933, in an appeal to the world's chiefs of state for practical disarmament, Roosevelt urged them to agree to eliminate all modern weapons of offense, which he listed as war planes, heavy mobile artillery, tanks, and poison gas (most of these having been proposed by the British). However, all post-First World War disarmament efforts foundered on the rock of dictatorship and fascism already loose in the world. The road to the Second World War was marked by Japan's seizure of Manchuria (1931-1932), Italy's conquest of Ethiopia (1935-1936), Nazi Germany's

The first US Navy-designed rigid airship, the ZR-1, later named the USS *Shenandoah,* seen (left) flying over St Louis, crashed in a storm near Ava, Ohio, on 3rd September 1925 *Below:* Billy Mitchell's charges of 'incompetency and criminal negligence' resulted in his court martial

reoccupation of the Rhineland (7th March 1936), and the outbreak of the Spanish Civil War (July 1936). In Spain, German air units of Hitler's Condor Legion on 26th April 1937 destroyed the town of Guernica, used, as Hermann Göring later testified, as 'a testing ground for the Luftwaffe.'

Two months after the bombing of Guernica, Japanese and Chinese forces clashed near Peking, signalling the start of an all-out campaign by Japan to eradicate what Tokyo declared was 'the anti-foreign and anti-Japanese movement rampant in China . . .' From the start of this campaign, the Japanese Air Force bombed and strafed numerous Chinese cities, including Nanking, Hankow, Nanyang, and Chungking. When American protests against these attacks were ignored by Japan, President Roosevelt suggested in an address to his countrymen on 5th October 1937 that the peaceful nations of the world might have to take steps to 'quarantine' the aggressors. The implications of his remarks led several isolationist senators and newspapers to call for his impeachment. The American Federation of Labor resolved against American involvement in any foreign wars.

Although worried about China, Roosevelt's primary attention was on Europe where Britain and France – paralyzed by their fears of the growing power of Germany – stood aside in

Of particular significance in the story of US bomber development was the Martin 123, or XB-907, which featured internal bomb stowage and offered – by contemporary standards – a phenomenal performance. The definitive production version, the B-10B (above right) provided the backbone of the Army Air Corps' bombing component until the late thirties. The Douglas DB-1, evolved in competition with the Boeing 299, was ordered into production as the B-18 (right), only an evaluation batch of the more revolutionary Boeing contender being contracted for

The Boeing 294 flew on 15th October, 1937 as the XB-15 (above and below),
it was the largest and heaviest aircraft built in the USA to that time. It proved
underpowered and served out its life as a cargo carrier until scrapped in 1945.
Right : The Boeing 299, prototype of the B-17 series, being rolled out prior to its
first test flight on 28th July, 1935. Subsequently referred to unofficially as the
'XB-17', in fact, no military designation was ever applied to this aircraft

March 1938 while Hitler incorporated Austria into the Third Reich. Six months later, at Munich, the victors of the First World War acquiesced in Hitler's dismemberment of the Czechoslovakian Republic. To many Americans, British and French appeasement of the German dictator seemed inexplicable. A member of Parliament, Winston Churchill, addressing the people of the United States in October 1938, gave a partial answer when he cited the 'grievous practical disadvantage' of Parliamentary societies facing totalitarian states, plus 'the blackmailing power of air-bombing . . .' The writer, Walter Lippman, was more explicit. Americans should ask themselves how they would feel, he said, if a powerful enemy air force was based less than one hour from Washington, New York, Boston, Detroit, Pittsburgh, and Chicago, 'believed to be capable of killing and wounding somewhere between 30,000 and 45,000 human beings in one raid.'

The development of the B-29 – and the atomic bomb – was a direct outgrowth of the traumatic events which took place in Europe in 1938 and after. President Roosevelt had noted the German dictator's use of the Luftwaffe as a weapon of political blackmail and he determined to strengthen America's air arm. In late September 1938, in one of his first moves to prepare the United States, he ordered a survey of the nation's aircraft industry to determine whether it could expand its capacity to manufacture 15,000 planes a year. He intended to build up US air power to the point where it could defend the nation and the Western Hemisphere against any aggressor or group of aggressors. According to Major-General Hap Arnold, then acting head of the Army Air Corps who was consulted at the White House on these matters, Roosevelt expressed the conviction that an air force was 'the only thing that Hitler understands.' The President's close adviser, Harry Hopkins, and General George C Marshall, soon to be named Army Chief of Staff, also became strong advocates of air power.

On 4th January 1939, in a message to

A two-gun power turret just aft of the flight deck, a remotely-sighted twin-gun
power turret in the fuselage belly, and a 'Stinger' turret in the tail cone characterised
the B-17E version of the Flying Fortress. The first B-17E (above) flew on 5th
September, 1941. A late production aircraft, a B-17F-70, on a mission over Europe is
seen below with bomb-bay doors open

A B-17F-100 (above) was fitted with a 'chin' turret and revised beam positions, this being considered sufficient to warrant a new series designation. It thus became protoype for the B-17G, last production version of the B-17 series, and was built in the greatest number. The first production version of the Flying Fortress, the B-17B (below), flew on 27th June, 1939, and thirty-nine were built for the Army Air Corps

Left: Major-General Henry H 'Hap' Arnold, an early advocate of the use of strategic heavy bombers. *Above:* The first of three XB-29 prototypes of the Superfortress. It flew at Seattle for the first time on 21st September 1942 with Edmund 'Eddie' Allen at the controls

Congress, the President explained why it was necessary to substantially increase America's air strength. The world, he said, had grown so small 'and weapons of attack so swift that no nation can be safe in its will to peace so long as any powerful nation refuses to settle its grievances at the council table. For if any government bristling with implements of war insists on policies of force, weapons of defence give the only safety.' Shortly after, Roosevelt sent a request to Congress for a $300 million appropriation to purchase 'several types of airplanes for the Army,' which would provide it a minimum increase of 3,000 airplanes. (At the time of Munich, the Air Corps inventory totalled about 1,800 aircraft, a third of which were obsolescent.)

After several months of debate – during which the isolationists in Congress dragged their feet until Hitler broke the deadlock by swallowing up the rest of Czechoslovakia – the legislators on 3rd April 1939 authorized the Army to purchase 3,000 new aircraft and raised the Air Corps authorized ceiling to 5,500 planes. The funds the appropriations committees later provided included the initial monies which the Air Corps used to start work on the B-29.

B-29 development

To begin the task of laying out a long-range aircraft development and production program, General Arnold sought the advice of knowledgeable airmen, including Charles A Lindbergh, just returned home in April 1939 after living in England and Europe for several years. While overseas, Lindbergh had toured German aircraft facilities at the invitation of Hermann Göring, observed Luftwaffe exercises, and came away quite impressed by Germany's air strength. Considered pro-Nazi by many of his countrymen at the time, he would later join the isolationists in arguing the United States should stay out of the European troubles. Arnold, however, was primarily interested in what Lindbergh had to say about German aeronautical advances. During their private conversations in the spring of 1939, Lindbergh restated that he had privately told Prime Minister Neville Chamberlain's government that Germany's air power was greater than that of all the European nations combined, and that Hitler held the destruction of any major city on the continent, or in Britain, in his hands.

Impressed by his knowledge of German technological developments, Arnold asked the famous flyer to serve on a board to determine what equipment the Air Corps should procure or develop as it proceeded to expand its forces. Lindbergh accepted the assignment and several days later reported for active duty as a Reserve Colonel. His first job was to tour the nation's aeronautical facilities, where he met with American aircraft builders and engineers, and discussed the latest advances in Europe. In early May 1939 he joined the special board, headed by Brigadier-General W G Kilner and including three other officers, all of whom later became generals, Lieutenant-Colonel Carl 'Toohey' Spaatz, Lieutenant-Colonel E L Naiden, and Major A J Lyon. Arnold directed the board to examine the military characteristics of all types of aircraft and recommend changes the Air Corps should make in its procurement and development programs.

The board began its work on 5th May and produced, by the end of June, a comprehensive report which outlined projects it proposed the Air Corps initiate in order to obtain advanced aircraft, weapons, and equipment by the year 1944. One of these

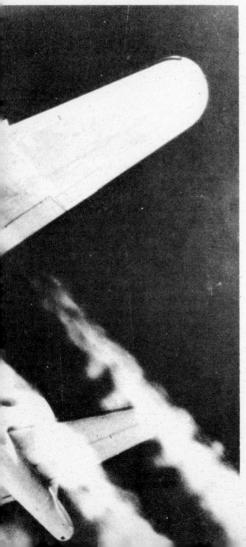

A B-17G Flying Fortress of the 8th Air Force, streaming contrails and with bomb-bay doors open, commences its run-up to the target, somewhere in Germany

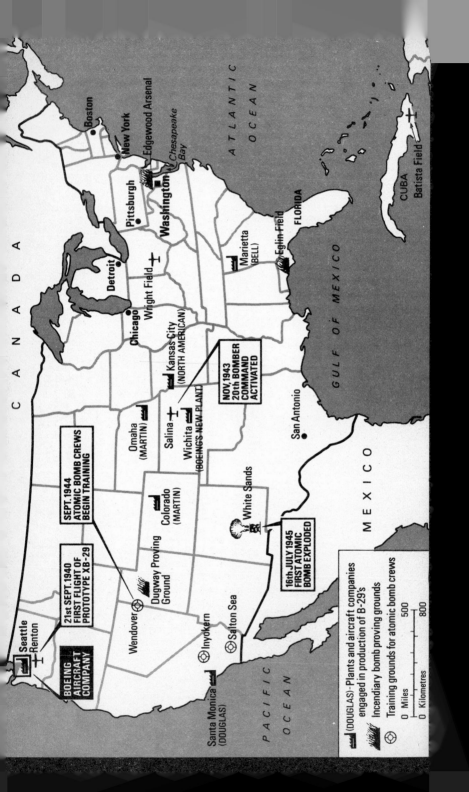

recommendations concerned the development of several long range medium and heavy bombers. The Kilner-Lindbergh report was still under review when, on 1st September 1939, Hitler started the Second World War with a massive air and ground assault against Poland. That same day President Roosevelt issued an appeal to all the belligerents to avoid 'the inhuman barbarism' of 'bombing from the air of civilians in unfortified centers . . .' (On 1st December he also appealed to the Soviet Union, then attacking Finland, to pledge it would not resort to aerial bombardment of civilians.) These appeals were made in vain. In the case of the brief battle for Poland, some 1,200 German fighters and bombers expeditiously destroyed the Polish Air Force, then went on to other tasks in support of Panzer Divisions, and in the process bombed Warsaw and other cities in Poland. On 17th September the country's fate was sealed when the Soviet Union invaded from the east. Ten days later, after it had undergone a severe air and artillery bombardment, Warsaw capitulated to the Germans. Throughout September and for many months after, Britain and France – having declared war on Germany but fearing to engage with the enemy in a mutual bombing of cities – limited themselves to dropping propaganda leaflets. As the Germans and Russians settled down to absorb their new conquest, there began that bleak period known in history as the 'phony war' of the winter of 1939-1940.

This was the background against which the Army Air Corps moved to acquire a very long range (VLR) heavy bomber. On 10th November 1939, Arnold formally requested authority to contract for studies of such an aircraft. Approval was given on 2nd December and instructions immediately were sent to Wright Field to draft a statement of desired military characteristics. The author of this document was Captain Donald L Putt, the test pilot and engineer officer who had survived the crash of the prototype B-17 in October 1935. On 29th January 1940, the completed statement was sent to various aircraft manufacturers with a 'request for data.' Four firms – Boeing, Lockheed Aircraft, Douglas, and Consolidated Aircraft – responded within a month's time with preliminary engineering design information and contract bids. This data arrived, however, after the Air Corps discovered – on the basis of the latest intelligence on combat air operations in Europe – that many existing American aircraft were dangerously obsolescent. All the belligerents appeared to be adopting leak-proof or armored fuel tanks or both. The French had withdrawn from their combat units several US pursuit and bomber aircraft until their fuel tanks could be given armor protection. The British were adding armor protection for their bomber crews and taking steps to beef up aircraft armament.

On the basis of this information, the Air Corps on 4th April 1940 requested the VLR bidders to resubmit their proposals to include provisions for leakproof tanks, armor plating, multiple gun turrets and heavier caliber guns and cannon. The revised bids, received at Wright Field in May, were evaluated by a board of officers headed by Colonel (later Major-General) Oliver P Echols, Chief of the Material Command. The board finally selected Boeing and Lockheed as the competition winners; the Boeing design (model 345), however, was considered the leading proposal. It contemplated an enormous aircraft with a wingspan of 141 feet and a fuselage 93 feet long. The bomber was expected to have a top speed of 382mph at 25,000 feet, a range of 7,000 miles, and be able to carry 2,000 pounds of bombs. In addition, it would mount ten .50 caliber machine guns in five positions, plus a 20mm cannon in the tail. The Air Corps designated Boeing's design the XB-29 and named Captain Putt Project Officer.

Major-General Carl 'Toohey' A Spaatz, an early proponent of the strategic bombing doctrine

Colonel Charles A Lindbergh, 'Lucky Lindy' was immensely impressed by the bombing capability of the Luftwaffe

On 4th June 1940 Arnold approved the award of contracts to Boeing and Lockheed to build wooden mockups of their designs and to test them in wind tunnels. He also directed the Materiel Command to negotiate prices and delivery of two prototypes from each manufacturer and to incorporate into the contracts an Air Corps option to purchase an additional two hundred bombers of each model. By 24th August, Boeing had completed investigations of its design in wind tunnel tests. Its report was accepted by the Air Corps and Arnold recommended to the Assistant Secretary of War, Robert J Patterson, that he approve an additional contract covering construction of a full-size wooden mockup and procurement of two XB-29s from Boeing, at a cost of $3,615,095.00. Patterson approved the proposed contract on 6th September 1940. Lockheed, on the other hand, at this time decided to abandon bombers in order to specialize in the manufacture of pursuit aircraft. Whereupon, the Air Corps awarded a parallel VLR bomber contract to a third bidder, Consolidated Aircraft, designating its design as the XB-32. This plane, however, never entered mass production and only fifteen would actually see action during the war.

During the nine month period between November 1939, when Arnold asked the War Department for authority to initiate the heavy bomber studies, and September 1940, when the XB-29 contract was awarded, the political map of Europe had been violently redrawn by Hitler's troops. In April 1940 his armed forces invaded and conquered Denmark and Norway and in May they smashed their way into Holland and Belgium. The Panzer/Luftwaffe combination proved as devastating in the Lowlands and France as it had in Poland. Reacting to these astounding and frightening events, President Roosevelt on 16th May sent a message to Congress calling for production of 50,000 warplanes a year, a proposal that seemed incredible

Brigadier-General Walter G Kilner, who headed a special board which analysed future Air Corps requirements

Brigadier-General Kenneth B Wolfe, closely associated with the development of the B-29, later referred to the Superfortress as a 'three billion dollar gamble'

since the Americans during the previous thirty-five years had built a total of no more than 40,000 planes. Roosevelt's decision to increase aircraft production had no effect whatever on events in Europe. By early June 1940 the British had managed to extricate the bulk of their troops from the beaches at Dunkirk. By 10th June, Paris was in Nazi hands and, with much of Europe under his control, Hitler waited for the British to sue for peace.

The President and his aides were greatly affected by the changed European scene. Their view of events, as expressed to a Congressional committee in August 1940 by the new Secretary of War, Henry L Stimson, was that:

'Air power today has decided the fate of nations. Germany with her powerful air armadas has vanquished one people after another. On the ground, large armies have been mobilized to resist her, but each time it was that additional power in the air that decided the fate of each individual nation . . . [As a consequence] we are in the midst of a great crisis. The time factor is our principal obstacle.'

With fears rising about America's own security, Air Corps planners – while the air battle of Britain raged in the summer and fall of 1940 – studied the use of long-range bombers in helping to defend the western hemisphere. Although the government had little hard intelligence about Hitler's specific intentions toward the Americas, its fears of the German leader's ambitions were not entirely groundless. In October 1940, during a conference with his naval commanders, Hitler discussed steps they might take to 'teach' the obviously pro-British Americans a lesson. He spoke of the possibilities of seizing the Azores as a base to directly attack the United States at a future date. Seven months later, at another conference with his naval commanders, Hitler again expressed himself as 'still in favor of occupying the Azores, in

27

Two weeks before the first of the three XB-29 Superfortress prototypes made its first flight at Seattle (above), the first prototype of a parallel strategic bomber development, the Convair XB-32 (right), had flown

order to be able to operate long-range bombers from there against the USA.' He suggested the occasion for this might arise by the autumn of 1941. However, by autumn he had given up his campaign to pound Britain into submission and had sent his military forces into a new and fatal misadventure against the Soviet Union. This changed situation led Air Corps planners to propose a new mission for the B-29s – striking at the heart of Germany from bases in Britain or the Mediterranean area.

Meanwhile, a board of officers in late November 1940 visited the Boeing plant at Seattle to inspect the full-scale wooden mockup of the B-29. They found it very impressive, complete and accurate and, in December, ordered a third prototype. As Boeing continued work on the plane, a number of airmen became concerned about its proposed radical wing design through which the firm sought to achieve an aerodynamic breakthrough. Its designers and engineers were faced with a major problem of air resistance since they intended to build a bomber with a gross weight of some 98,000 pounds – more than twice the weight of the B-17 – drive it through the air approximately thirty percent faster, and yet use only eighty-three percent more horsepower. To obtain the required performance, Boeing decided to increase the load borne by each square foot of surface (overall wing area 1,739 square feet) to double that of the B-17. This, however, would produce a very fast landing speed. To make the landings manageable, the firm's designers then proceeded to devise a huge flap covering 332 feet of area – larger than the entire wing of many a fighter aircraft – to enable the bomber to make slower landings by giving the wing more area and lift.

A long, thin, low-drag wing finally emerged from the above effort and contributed significantly to the B-29s remarkable performance. Boeing also sought to produce an aerodynamically clean plane. It made all rivets flush, used butt-joints instead of overlaps, and folded the landing gear flat up into the wing. Since the last item required a much stronger wing, the firm abandoned the traditional bridge-type truss structure and adopted web-type construction employing spars made of flat plates of sheet metal, with the flanges bent up for rigidity. For the tail, Boeing selected, after an exhaustive investigation, a

tail developed for the B-17E which it modified slightly in size only.

The installation of a cabin supercharger was another important innovation. Its flow capacity of twenty-five pounds per minute provided a pressurized B-29 cabin inside atmosphere equivalent to 8,000 feet at an actual altitude of 30,000 feet. Boeing previously had built the world's first pressurized commercial transport, the Stratoliner. The B-29, however, presented a special problem in that it would have two large bomb bay doors which would be repeatedly opened and closed. The designers solved this problem by pressurizing the forward control cabin and the gunners compartment toward the rear of the plane, and connecting the two with a long tube, thirty-four inches in diameter, just large enough for an airman to crawl through.

To power the B-29, the Air Corps selected the Wright R-3350 eighteen cylinder, air-cooled engine, which produced 2,200 horsepower at takeoff. Design work on this engine had begun in January 1936. The first model completed a successful fifty hour endurance run in April 1937, when it produced 1,500 horsepower. By adding a supercharger, Wright engineers were able to increase its output to 2,200 horsepower. In June 1941, a month after the government advised Boeing that it intended to purchase 250 B-29s, the Air Corps formally adopted the Wright engine as the bomber's power plant, although at the time only one R-3350 was available. The engine, however, was not fully developed when the first production aircraft began coming off the production lines and, for a time, its repeated failures threatened to undermine the entire B-29 program.

As work on the bomber proceeded,

The second XB-32 flew on 2nd July 1943 – the first crashing after thirty flights – but the success of the B-29 had already made the Convair bomber redundant in the high-altitude role

31

Part of the immense Boeing plant at Seattle where B-17 Flying Fortresses were under construction. To avoid any disruption of the B-17 programme Boeing had to build a new plant at Wichita, Kansas, to manufacture the B-29 Superfortress

many design changes were made – 900 between the time the XB-29 design was first approved in the spring of 1940 and the date of its first test flight in late 1942. One of the more important changes followed the belated decision of the newly-formed AAF (Army Air Forces, successor to the Air Corps, effective 20th June 1941) in late 1941 to incorporate a completely new armament system, designed by the General Electric Company, into the plane. Because the change was made at such a late date in the B-29's development, the first flight of the prototype slipped by

several months. The new armament system included a small automatic computer, which corrected for range, altitude, temperature, and airspeed, and a central control mechanism which enabled any gunner, except the tail gunner, to take over more than one of the five power-driven, 50 caliber turrets at one time. A gunner without a target within his field of vision could pass control of his turret to another crewman who could use it. With this system, the gunners also were physically removed from manual contact with their guns and, except for the tail gunner, fired them from remote stations, this spared them the jar and vibration of recoil, made it easier to track an enemy aircraft, and to hold the sights on it.

The pressurization system, the fire control system, specially designed four-bladed Hamilton propellers, and hundreds of other minor but important engineering advances incorporated into the plane demanded increased amounts of electric power. Since existing generator equipment did not have the required capacity, entirely new B-29 electric motors had to be designed. Eventually, more than 125 of these were installed in the bomber, which added substantially to its overall weight. A B-29 weight reduction board was later formed and recommended removal of superfluous instruments, auxiliary crew bunks, cabin sound proof lining, and redesign of a number of major components. The final gross weight of the plane came to 105,000 pounds.

In May 1941, when Washington informed Boeing it intended to purchase 250 B-29s, it directed the firm to procure jigs, dies, fixtures, and critical materiel and equipment needed to produce the bomber and spare parts. Boeing immediately began expanding its work force and production facilities. On 24th June 1941, it broke ground at Wichita, Kansas, for a new plant to be devoted solely to production of the new aircraft. The government contract for the initial order – which Brigadier-General Kenneth B Wolfe of the Materiel Command later termed 'a three billion dollar gamble' on an airplane, which had yet to make its first test flight – was signed on 6th September. Following the 7th December 1941 Japanese attack on Pearl Harbor, the B-29 order was increased to 500 planes.

This was but the first of a series of new orders for the bomber. On 10th February 1942, representatives of the AAF, the aircraft industry, the War Production Board, and others met in Detroit, Michigan, and decided to produce 1,600 B-29s at four separate facilities. Boeing was made responsible not only for its own production facilities, but also for furnishing the three other contractors – General Motors' Fisher Division, North American Aviation, and the Bell Aircraft Corporation – control master gauges, detailed forging dies, extru-

sion dies, patterns, and templates. The Fisher Division was assigned the production of all forgings, castings, and stampings required by Bell and North American and was directed to provide complete B-29 sub-assemblies such as tail surfaces, flaps, wing tips, and complete engine nacelles. Bell and North American were responsible for building bomb center sections and fuselages, and assembling the airplanes in final form at plants at Marietta, Georgia, and Kansas City, Missouri, respectively. Two other plants – Boeing's Renton, Washington, facility and the Martin Company's Omaha, Nebraska, assembly line – were later brought into the B-29 production consortium.

In addition to the above agreements, the conferees formed a B-29 Liaison Committee, headed by General Wolfe and including representatives of the contractors and the War Production Board. In late April 1942 the Committee adopted a formal charter and established an executive unit which was given full powers to make decisions, except for contractual matters, to be binding on all parties involved in B-29 production. Wolfe, the key man in the coordination process, organized a number of subcommittees to implement Committee decisions. As he became more and more identified with the B-29 in Arnold's mind, he emerged as the logical man to take the first combat crews into action two years later.

While these production plans were being implemented, top AAF officials anxiously awaited the first test flight of the prototype. In early September 1942, XB-29 number one was moved out to Boeing Field, next to the factory. On the 9th its test pilot, Edmund T Allen, winner of the 1939 Chanute award for notable contributions to aeronautical sciences, ran up its four engines and began taxi tests. On 15th September he lifted the prototype off the runway three times to approximately fifteen feet altitude. During these preliminary tests, it became apparent that the Wright engines could scarcely operate an hour before showing distress. They were changed frequently (although no more than thirty engines were available by October) and finally, on 21st September 1942, the XB-29 took off on a seventy-five minute flight. When it landed, a smiling Eddie Allen emerged to proclaim the B-29 an excellent plane. The next day the Project Officer, now Colonel Putt, took the XB-29 up for the government and confirmed Allen's report. In his notes Putt jotted down the following comments: 'Unbelievable for such large plane to be so easy on controls . . . easier to fly than B-17 . . . faster than any previous heavy bomber . . . control forces very light . . . stall characteristics remarkable for heavy plane . . .'

During the next several months the test flights continued to check out various sytems. On 2nd December, after having accumulated nearly eighteen hours flight time, the plane was taken up to 25,000 feet for the first time. During the month Allen and his crew compiled data on the minimum distance for B-29 takeoffs and landings at various gross weights. As the tests continued, it became clear the plane would easily meet its specifications, provided the engines performed properly. Thus, for example, on 28th December – on its twenty-second flight, the plane's number one engine failed completely and forced Allen to return to the field. Ground inspection revealed a second engine also had failed; both were removed and replaced. On 30th December, during the maiden flight of XB-29 number two, fire broke out in one of its engines at 3,000 feet altitude and the test was suspended.

Despite these troubles, important and vital data on the plane's performance continued to accumulate. In January, when the first prototype was laid up for numerous repairs, Allen continued flight tests with the second XB-29. Then, on 18th February 1943, during another flight with the second

plane to check out power plant and other airplane performance, there was a disaster. Eight minutes after the XB-29 got airborne, a fire broke out in the number one nacelle, but was quickly smothered by the fire extinguishing system. Allen decided to head back to Boeing Field and began descending for a landing, when a fire started in the number two nacelle and quickly spread into the wing. As several pieces of burning metal fell off, the B-29 went into a steeply banked attitude and crashed into the fifth floor of a brick building, three miles from the end of the Boeing runway, and exploded. Allen and his entire test crew of ten men were killed. Nineteen people in the building and one fireman also died as a result of the crash.

It was the second crackup of a Boeing prototype bomber in seven years. In 1935 the firm had lost its lead test pilot in the XB-17 crash. Now, the much-admired Allen and his expert test crew were dead. When the bad news reached Washington, Arnold ordered an immediate investigation and specifically directed that steps be taken to isolate the engine fires. In March and April 1943, a Senate investigating committee, headed by Senator Harry S Truman of Missouri, initiated its own inquiry. The committee found that the manufacturer had produced many defective and substandard power plants, that there had been careless inspection of completed engines as the firm's management emphasized production (orders for the R-3350 had been increased to more than 40,000) rather than quality, and that the AAF was partially to blame for the situation. While the investigations continued, the entire B-29 program slowed to a crawl.

During the crisis a B-29 flight test officer at Wright Field, Colonel Leonard 'Jake' Harman, proposed to General Wolfe that a special organization be formed to take over the entire program, including production, flight tests, training, and getting the bom-

The first production B-29 Superfortress rolling off the assembly line at Boeing's new Wichita plant late in 1943

bers into action at the earliest possible date. Wolfe agreed and, in mid-April, the two men flew to Washington to present the plan to Arnold. Several days later, on 18th April, the AAF chief approved the proposal and authorized them to organize the 'B-29 Special Project', with Wolfe as its head and Harman his deputy. They were directed to take charge of the flight test program and the training of the crews so that the B-29 could be committed to combat by late 1943.

Wolfe and Harman proceeded at once to Seattle, where they arranged for the AAF to take over prototype test flights. On 29th May, more than three months after the crash of the XB-29, Harman prepared to take up the third prototype – and the plane was almost wrecked. Through an incredible oversight in the factory, the aileron control cables on the plane had been reversed. While Wolfe and two Boeing officials watched, Harman roared down the field, but instead of rising the plane's right wing went

down as it banked sharply and the XB-29 careened on down the strip and disappeared behind some buildings. When the three white-faced officials reached the scene, they found the plane undamaged and a shaken test pilot. A check quickly uncovered the crossed wires. The B-29 project – which possibly might have been doomed by a second crash – escaped disaster by a whisker. The lesson of this incident was drummed into the heads of every production worker in Boeing's plants in the days that followed.

During subsequent test flights, the Wright engines continued to malfunction. Between February 1943 and September 1944, at least nineteen B-29 accidents were attributed to engine fire problems. Corrective steps were taken to eliminate the problems, but the R-3350 engine was still not ready for combat when the planes were sent overseas.

Planning
the bombing
of Japan:
1940-1943

In the spring of 1943 Wolfe was named commander of the newly activated 58th Bombardment Wing and directed to prepare the B-29s for possible deployment to China by year's end to begin the bombing of Japan. The decision to use them in the Far East was President Roosevelt's. As early as December 1940, a year before Pearl Harbor, he had expressed the hope to see the Japanese bombed. For more than three years, they had been assailing China on land and in the air. Japanese bombers had struck repeatedly at Chungking, the western refuge of the Nationalist government of President Chiang Kai-shek. The US ambassador in Chungking, Nelson T Johnson, by the summer of 1939 had personally undergone sixty-six of the aerial attacks. To Washington's protests about the indiscriminate raids, the Japanese responded that their forces were directed only against enemy military targets.

The exasperated US government in late 1939 decided to retaliate by embargoing the sale of aviation products to Japan and further it announced it would not renew the Treaty of Commerce and Navigation signed with Tokyo in 1911, which would expire on 26th January 1940. The day after the expiration, Secretary of State Cordell Hull handed the Japanese Ambassador in Washington a letter listing more than thirty-five Chinese cities which had been bombed by Japanese aircraft and the specific dates of certain ones. He further cited approximately 200 instances in China 'of damage by aerial bombs to American properties, the location of the majority of which were previously notified to the Japanese authorities and nearly all of which were marked by American flags.'

As for Japan's denials that it had bombed targets other than 'the warlike organizations and establishments of the Chinese,' Hull declared that: 'detailed reports have come to this country, some official and some by way of private sources and the public press, which indicate that in their military operations in China the Japanese forces have in a large number of instances resorted to bombing and machine-gunning of civilians from the air at places near which there were no military establishments or organizations. Furthermore, the use of incendiary bombs (which inevitably and ruthlessly jeopardize non-military persons and properties) has inflicted appalling losses on civilian populations. Japanese air attacks in many instances have been of a nature and apparent plan which can be comprehended only as constituting deliberate attempts to terrorize unarmed populations.'

It was not only Japan's aerial assault on China that troubled the Americans in the months that follow-

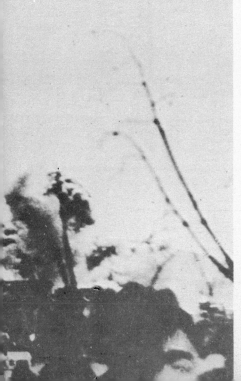

Between May and September 1940 Japanese Navy bombers made 168 day and 14 night attacks on Chungking. The photograph left was taken at the height of one of the day attacks

Bodies of Chinese civilians piled outside a Chungking air raid shelter in which 700 people lost their lives

ed, but Tokyo's growing cockiness and appetite for new territories, stimulated by the brilliant German victories in Europe. Hitler's successes went to Japanese heads 'like strong wine'. Thus, they not only continued their bombing of Chungking and other Chinese cities but, on 14th June 1940, informed the American ambassador in Tokyo that they intended 'to increase hereafter the severity of these attacks' and could not accept responsibility for injuries suffered by any American officials or US nationals who remained in Chinese territory.

Further, on 20th June – with Paris under Nazi occupation – they browbeat French officials in Indochina into agreeing to the stationing of Japanese 'inspectors' along the Indochina railroad to prevent the shipment of war materials to China. Also, on 18th July, in response to a veiled threat from Tokyo, the beleaguered British agreed to halt the shipment of war materials to Chiang Kai-shek's forces through Burma and Hong Kong (a decision they rescinded in October). Finally, in the early fall of 1940, the Japanese joined Germany and Italy in a ten-year military-economic alliance, whose proclaimed goal was 'to establish and maintain a new order of things' in Europe and Asia.

These were among the events which led the President to express the wish that the Chinese somehow might bomb Japan. Secretary Hull, as angry with the Japanese as Roosevelt, had an alternate idea. On 10th December 1940, during a conference with Secretary of the Treasury Henry Morgenthau, he suggested the United States should get 500 planes, start them from the Aleutians, and fly over Japan 'just once' – and perhaps 'drop some bombs on Tokyo' – to teach the Japanese a lesson. However, it was the President's

words that Morgenthau had taken to heart. He broached the subject to the Chinese Foreign Minister in Washington, T V Soong, and later discussed it with General P T Mow of the Chinese Air Force, and Colonel Claire L Chennault, a former US Air Corps pilot and an adviser to Chiang Kai-shek. Mow and Chennault had arrived in Washington in late November 1940 as emissaries of Chiang to seek 500 American fighter planes and pilots to come to China's aid.

When Morgenthau, whose department was responsible for coordinating aircraft procurement programs, proposed giving the Chinese some B-17s – with the proviso that the bombers be used to attack Tokyo and other Japanese cities – they were delighted. A telegram to Chiang brought prompt acceptance of the Morgenthau proposal. Whereupon, in mid-December, Morgenthau, Mow, and Chennault met to discuss the project further and to examine maps, with Chennault pointing out the bases in China from which the B-17s could strike Japan. On 19th December 1940 Morgenthau presented the plan to the President and several members of the Cabinet and received Roosevelt's enthusiastic endorsement. On 22nd December, however, the entire proposal was shot down during a meeting at the home of Secretary of War Stimson, attended by Morgenthau, General Marshall, and the Secretary of the Navy, Frank Knox. Marshall argued that the United States did not have enough Flying Fortresses for its own forces and had already been required by the President to send a number of the B-17s to Britain. Morgenthau immediately accepted Marshall's judgement and, in lieu of the long-range bombers, they agreed to let the Chinese have 100 pursuit planes. Although disappointed, Chiang Kai-shek was glad to accept the alternate offer and, during the early months of 1941, Chennault busied himself with the task of recruiting

Generalissimo and Madame Chiang Kai-shek with Lieutenant-General Joseph W Stilwell at Maymo, Burma on 9th April 1942. Stilwell disagreed with Chennault that emphasis in China should be placed on air operations

US officers to join an American Volunteer Group in China, which later achieved fame as the 'Flying Tigers'.

The idea of the retaliatory bombing of course, received fervent support following the Japanese attack on Pearl Harbor. However, between 7th December 1941 and the spring of 1942 the armed forces of the Empire swept all before them. In an extraordinary series of military operations extending over hundreds of thousands of miles, they seized many new, rich territories including the Philippines, the Netherland East Indies, and Borneo. They also occupied Hong Kong, Singapore, and Rangoon, drove the Allies from Burma, closed the Burma road, captured Guam, Wake, and the Gilbert Islands, and invaded Attu and Kiska in the Aleutians. Only the surprise raid on Tokyo on 18th April 1942 by carrier-launched B-25 twin-engine bombers led by Colonel James H Doolittle lifted the Allied gloom.

Doolittle's raid was lauded in

may cut the Burma road, but I want to say to the gallant people of China that no matter what advances the Japanese may make, ways will be found to deliver airplanes and munitions of war to the armies of Generalissimo Chiang Kai-shek. We remember that the Chinese people were the first to stand up and fight against the aggressors in this war.'

Determined to 'keep China in the war and to hold the friendship of the Chinese people for the United States', Roosevelt authorized an airlift from India over the Himalayas to China to help supply Chiang's forces and Chennault's air units, soon reformed as the Fourteenth Air Force. Later, in January 1943 – at the Casablanca conference with Prime Minister Churchill and the Combined Chiefs of Staff – the President supported a plan recommended by General Joseph W Stilwell, Chiang's chief of staff, that the Allies begin preparations for a ground offensive to recapture Burma. Intermittently throughout the Casablanca conference the Americans and British discussed the possibility of bombing Japan. General Marshall voiced the AAF's view of the matter, declaring that the Japanese industries were 'so vulnerable to the air that heavy attack would destroy her capacity to maintain her war effort.'

Roosevelt agreed, but he also saw the 'periodic bombing of Japan' as having 'a tremendous morale effect on the Chinese people'. During a discussion of the subject on 18th January, the President specifically suggested sending 200 to 300 planes to China, including heavy bombers. Recognizing the great problem in supplying them, he proposed that the bombers be based in India and used 'to operate in raids over Japan proper by refueling in China on their way to and from such missions'. Marshall cautioned that supplying the bombers in China would be 'tremendously expensive' and would require air transport planes that were needed elsewhere. However, the President insisted that they

America, but it was the Chinese who paid the bill. In an angry reaction, the Japanese launched a massive offensive on the mainland which drove 200 miles through the heart of East China, devastated some 20,000 square miles, ploughed up landing fields, and exterminated everyone remotely suspected of aiding the Doolittle flyers. The populations of entire villages through which the Americans passed were slaughtered and their houses burned to the ground. Much concerned about China's feeble resistance, the President on 28th April publicly pledged to the Chinese government his continued support: 'The Japanese

Above: General George C Marshall with General Dwight D Eisenhower during a meeting in North Africa in September, 1943. He voiced the AAF's view that Japanese industry was 'so vulnerable to the air that heavy attack would destroy her capacity to maintain her war effort'. *Below:* President Roosevelt and Prime Minister Winston Churchill, seen during the Atlantic conference, August, 1941. *Right:* Major - General Claire L Chennault and Brigadier - General Edgar E Glenn, Kunming, China, 3rd November. 1944

Secretary of the US Treasury Henry Morgenthau proposed in 1940 that the Chinese be given B-17 Flying Fortresses

US Secretary of State Cordell Hull suggested that the US bomb Tokyo from the Aleutians

President Franklin D Roosevelt fully appreciated the use that Germany was making of its newly-created Luftwaffe

must help China and, toward the end of the conference, he wired Chiang Kai-shek that he was sending General Arnold to Chungking to discuss US aid because he was 'determined to increase General Chennault's air force in order that you may carry the offensive to the Japanese at once'.

However, in the months that followed, Anglo-American plans for European operations kept intruding and taking the greater portion of the resources of the United States. Roosevelt, who was in complete agreement with Churchill that the defeat of Nazi Germany should be given top priority, found during 1943 that he was unable to provide the massive military assistance which the China-Burma-India (CBI) theater required. In the meantime, Stilwell and Chennault engaged in a serious quarrel over strategy in China. Both men accepted the premise (which proved erroneous) that, as Stilwell put it, 'We have to have China to get at Japan. If we are going to bomb Japan, we will have to have the China bases.' However, Chennault felt the Allies should emphasize air operations against Japanese forces in China, whereas Stilwell argued that, until powerful Chinese army divisions existed, the enemy would be able to launch offensives such as those that followed the Doolittle raid and would seize the Allied air bases on the mainland. First priority, Stilwell said, should be given to building up the Chinese army. Their dispute was presented to Roosevelt just prior to the Trident conference in Washington in May 1943. The President decided he would back Chennault, whose proposed air campaign seemed to offer hope of giving immediate help to Chungking. He authorized an increase in airlift over the Hump to support this campaign.

The B-29 did not enter the planning picture until the Quadrant conference of Allied leaders at Quebec in August 1943. At this meeting, Arnold submitted an 'Air Plan for the Defeat of Japan' prepared by Wolfe for use of the new bombers, the first production models of which came off the assembly lines in July. He proposed deploying the B-29s to Central China, possibly around the city of Changsha. With their 1,500 mile operational range, he said they would be able to begin a sustained bombing campaign against Japan's war-making industries. To support the China bases, the AAF planned to convert a number of aircraft into transports to help carry supplies over the Hump to China. The Air Plan proposed to use Calcutta as the port of entry for the aviation fuel, bombs, and other war materials the B-29s would need. Although Arnold and his staff recognised that once the bombing raids got under way – projected for some time in October 1944 – the Japanese would launch attacks against the bomber bases, they assumed the Chinese army and Chennault's air units would be able to cope with the enemy.

The theory behind this air plan was straight out of the Billy Mitchell tradition and the Air Corps Tactical School's view of the proper role of air power. Via strategic bombardment, the airmen believed, US air power could smash Japan's war industries into impotency, neutralize its air forces, and destroy sufficient enemy naval and merchant ships to bring about a surrender. The air planners estimated that 780 B-29s – flying five missions a month – could complete the job of destruction in six months. They declared they could damage the enemy sufficiently to permit an Allied occupation of Japan by the end of August 1945 – which would fulfil the Combined Chiefs of Staff projected goal of defeating the Japanese twelve months after Germany's surrender.

Stilwell and his air commander in the CBI, Lieutenant-General George E Stratemeyer, were asked to evaluate the AAF plan. After studying it, they revised the plan to conform more to the suggestion first made by the President at Casablanca. That is, they proposed basing the B-29s in the Calcutta area and shuttling them forward to advanced bases in China where they would off-load some of their excess gasoline, load up with bombs, and head for Japan. The rear base concept had the advantage of providing security for the bombers as well as easing their maintenance problems. This altered plan, which was designated 'Matterhorn', was approved by Washington as the most feasible way to employ the B-29s until greater Allied resources could be made available in the theater.

Subsequently, the President on 10th November 1943 – just prior to the Allied conference at Cairo to which he had invited Chiang Kai-shek – sent a message to Churchill advising that:

'We have under development a project whereby we can strike a heavy blow at our enemy in the Pacific early next year with our new heavy bombers. Japanese military, naval and shipping strength is dependent upon the steel industry which is strained to the limit. Half of the coke for that steel can be reached and destroyed by long-range bombers operating from the Chengtu area of China. The bombers can supply themselves by air, from bases to be constructed near Calcutta, without disturbing present airlift commitments...

'In order to expedite this project I ask you to arrange for the Government of India to render every possible assistance in the construction of these four air bases for long range bombers...

'This is a bold but entirely feasible project. Together by this operation, we can partially cripple the Japanese naval and military power and hasten the victory of our forces in Asia.'

That same day, 10th November, Roosevelt wired Chiang to request the construction of five bomber fields in the Chengtu area, to insure their readiness by the end of March 1944. He said the United States would provide engineering advisers and he asked the Chinese government to supply the necessary labor and materials so as to avoid dipping into the vital air supply

Left: Smoke rises from one of Doolittle's Japanese targets. *Below:* One of Doolittle's sixteen B-25B Mitchells leaves the deck of the carrier *Hornet* en route to Japan, 18th April 1942

lines over the Hump. The President said: 'I am personally convinced we can deal the Jap a truly crippling blow, so close to our hearts, by this sudden, surprise attack.' Both Churchill and Chiang responded promptly and favorably, whereupon on 14th November the War Department issued movement orders to aviation engineers and dump truck companies required to build the India fields. The first contingent arrived in the subcontinent ten days later.

On 29th November 1943 the President also handed to Premier Joseph Stalin, during their Teheran conference, a letter inquiring as to the possibility of basing 'from 100 to 1,000 four-engine bombers' in the Soviet maritime provinces to attack Japan 'immediately after the start of hostilities between the USSR and Japan,' which he had pledged. Roosevelt asked that the US military mission in Moscow be provided information concerning airports, housing, supplies, communications, and weather in the maritime provinces. He also requested Stalin's permission to send 'a very few individuals' to conduct a physical survey of the territory, to be accomplished 'with the utmost secrecy'. Months elapsed before the Soviet leader responded to Roosevelt's request. But when he finally announced that the Soviet Union was prepared to let the United States put B-29 bases in Kamchatka, it still proved a will-of-the-wisp. As so often happened in Washington's dealings with Moscow, the Russians kept finding reasons for delay and the plan to base the bombers in the Soviet provinces was never implemented. The Russians, however, did manage to get to see – and to seize – a number of B-29s, as will be related in another chapter.

The battle of Kansas

Several weeks before he sailed for Cairo, the President had been told by Arnold that the new bombers would not be ready to deploy to China by 1st January 1944, a date the AAF commander had optimistically given to General Marshall months earlier. Upset by the news that the B-29s could not be deployed 'until March or April of next year', Roosevelt wrote to Marshall on 15th October 1943 to express his disgust with the India-China situation in general and Arnold's report in particular. Everything seemed to be going wrong, the President complained, but 'the worst thing is that we are falling down on our promises [to China] every single time.' Aware of Roosevelt's dissatisfaction, Arnold and his staff studied actions they might take to insure that at least 150 bombers were deployed to China by 15th April so that the bombing of Japan could begin on 1st May 1944.

One action taken on 2nd November 1943 was a request from Arnold to the US Joint Chiefs of Staff that top priority be assigned to B-29 production. The JCS referred the matter to the Joint Aircraft Committee, the agency responsible for approving and coordinating all aircraft contracts for military purchasers. However, after the Committee and the AAF had studied the matter, they concluded that program delays were caused not by shortages of materials or manpower, but were inherent in the manufacture of a new advanced aircraft. Assigning top priority to the B-29 would not speed the manufacturing process.

Another action Arnold took, in late November, was to activate the 20th Bomber Command under General Wolfe. This new combat organization, with headquarters at Smoky Hill Army Air Field, Salina, Kansas, was initially assigned two wings, the 58th and 73rd, each controlling several bombardment groups with twenty-eight B-29s to each group. To command the 58th Bombardment Wing, Wolfe selected his deputy on the B-29 Special Project, Colonel Harman. Named to lead the 73rd Wing was Colonel Thomas H Chapman, later succeeded by Brigadier-General Emmett 'Rosie' O'Donnell. The 73rd was later reassigned to the 21st

Colonel Leonard 'Jake' Harman, (left), co-pilot of the B-17B Flying Fortress that, in the summer of 1939, flew from Seattle to New York in 9hrs 14mins at an average speed of 265mph, establishing a new class record. He is seen here with some of the first personnel assigned to the B-29 training programme

Bomber Command. Responsibility for the aircrew training program, conducted by the Second Air Force, was assigned to La Verne G 'Blondie' Saunders, a B-17 pilot who had led combat missions against the Japanese at Guadalcanal.

Wolfe prepared a plan to train 452 combat crews. At least one hundred of these were to serve as replacements or in the B-29 training program. Each bomber would have an eleven-man crew which included five officers: a pilot-commander, co-pilot, two navigator-bombardiers, and a flight engineer. Enlisted personnel included three specialists who were responsible for electrical systems, the power plant, and the central fire-control system, and an engine mechanic (all four trained as gunners), plus radio and radar operators. This eleven-man crew – and in particular the presence of the flight engineer – was unique in the AAF. The flight engineer, who also could serve as third pilot, was responsible for the B-29's mechanical functioning, which freed the aircraft commander and co-pilot to concentrate on flying. Another unusual feature of the 20th Bomber Command was that it was provided with double crews for each plane, which gave the wings a very high percentage of commissioned personnel – 3,045 officers, with eight warrant officers, and 8,099 enlisted personnel.

When the pilots and aircraft specialists slowly began trickling into their Kansas bases in late 1943 to begin crew training, they were disappointed to find that the marvelous B-29s they had heard so much about were rare birds indeed. Because of production delays, the aircraft were in such short supply that, by the end of December, only sixty-seven 'first pilots' had managed to complete checkout flights and only one B-29 had flown on a long-range training mission. The average crew as of 31st December 1943 had accumulated only eighteen to thirty hours B-29 flight time, one-half of that in formation

flying below 20,000 feet, and none at the planned higher bombing altitudes.

Because of the B-29 shortage, the AAF was forced to substitute B-24s and B-17s for certain flight training. The B-17 was especially helpful because its mechanical parts were similar to those of the B-29 and also because the crews could fly reasonably long-range high altitude missions with them. The B-17s were used at altitudes of 20,000 feet in various simulated strikes, which 'bombed' out of existence the industrial heart of many a midwestern city. When B-29s became available, they were used in bombing missions which were 'intercepted' by P-47s and P-51s simulating attacks from

When B-29s became available intensive simulated bombing missions were performed in which the Superfortresses were 'intercepted' by AAF fighters. P-47 Thunderbolts frequently stood in for Japanese fighters, a P-47D-II being seen right, and a P-47D-25 with 'bubble' hood below

every conceivable angle to give the crews experience in the best defensive formations and most effective evasive tactics. Almost all bomber crews made long flights to Florida and Batista Field, Cuba, from where they practiced overwater navigation and simulated bombing missions.

While crew training was getting under way, Wolfe was concentrating on the problems he would find in the war zone. To obtain information on conditions there, in October 1943 he dispatched Colonel William F Fisher as his special emissary to China. Fisher was given a 'cover' assignment as commander of the 308th Bombardment Group, Fourteenth Air Force. He formally took over command of the group on 2nd November 1943 and led its B-24s into combat against the Japanese. In between these missions, he visited various base sites in China and conferred with Generals Stratemeyer and Chennault. The information collected he dispatched back to 20th Bomber Command via normal mail channels.

In November Wolfe sent another advanced party of five officers to India, where base construction was getting under way. With the help of the theater commander, Vice-Admiral Lord Louis Mountbatten, and the Central Public Works Department of India, US aviation engineers began work on several existing runways near Calcutta. Two members of the advanced party, shortly after their arrival in India in December, flew to Kunming, China, to consult with Chennault and Fisher on various operational matters. During this trip they arranged to procure escape and evasion information and such indispensables as money belts, silk maps, local currency, Chinese-Burmese

North American's P-51 Mustang was to figure prominently in the B-29's career *Left:* the first Merlin-engined Mustang, the P-51 B. *Above left:* A drop tank-equipped P-51 D of the type that escorted the B-29 over Japan

blood-chits, and other items needed by downed crews.

In Washington, meanwhile, Arnold grew anxious about the progress of the B-29 project and summoned Wolfe and Saunders to brief him in person. During this meeting on 21st December, in answer to Arnold's query, Wolfe reported he had only a handful of men in the theater, whereupon the AAF commander directed him to 'get over there yourself, with a few of your staff' to get a feel of the situation. Returning to Salina, Wolfe closed down his affairs, left Saunders in charge, and on 30th December departed the United States for India. He arrived in New Delhi on 13th January 1944 with five officers and ten enlisted men. Shortly thereafter, he began a whirl-wind tour of base sites in India and China. In China he completed arrangements for extending three existing Chengtu airstrips – at Hsinching, Pengshan, and Kiunglai – and construction of a fourth runway at Kwanghan. Actual work on the China bases began on 24th January. In an effort to accelerate the construction of the India bases, Wolfe also flew into the Burma jungles to Stilwell's headquarters in February. Once there, he somehow persuaded the tough infantry commander to loan him temporarily several Army construction battalions then working on Stilwell's high-priority Ledo road.

In all, some 6,000 US construction troops – more than half of them aviation engineers – plus thousands of Indian laborers worked on airstrips at Kharagpur, Chakulia, Piardoba, and Dudhkundi. There were many delays, caused by heat, dust, rain, mud, and a complicated Allied command arrangement, which made it necessary for 20th Bomber Command officials to seek authorizations and support from British, Indian, and US agencies. The result was that only two bases were barely operational by 30th April 1944 and it was not until September that all four were completed. Meanwhile, in China, hundreds of thousands

of peasants, working under the direction of US engineers, were slowly laying out the forward bases around Chengtu. Lacking modern equipment, the Chinese used baskets, wheel barrows, occasionally a cart, and sheer muscle power to haul tons of rock, gravel, and sand from nearby streams to build four 8,500-foot runways, nineteen inches thick. In addition, they helped construct fighter strips for Chennault's 315th Fighter Wing, which was assigned to defend the B-29 bases against Japanese attack.

As base construction moved slowly forward in the theater, in the United States the B-29 program became bogged down. Ninety-seven bombers had emerged from the factories by mid-January 1944, but only sixteen were flyable. Most of the others went from production lines to modification centers, some for as long as sixty days, so that hundreds of engineering changes – which grew out of the extended flight tests of the XB-29 – could be made. These modifications included the installation of additional bomb bay fuel cells and new parts of the AN/APQ-13 radar system, replacing training engines with 'war' engines, providing an installation of engine dollies and slings to permit each plane to carry a spare engine overseas and other changes. As a consequence, as of 15th January, 20th Bomber Command did not possess a single B-29 equipped for combat, and the scheduled delivery of 150 planes by early March seemed impossible.

Faced with the unhappy prospect of being unable to meet his new deadline and fulfilling his promise to the President, Arnold in mid-February flew to Marietta, Georgia, a major B-29 modification center, to take a

General Joseph W Stilwell, C-in-C of the US Forces in China, Burma, and India, at Myitkyina Airfield, northern Burma, a few hours after it was captured from the Japanese on 17th May 1944

personal look into the situation. After he was briefed by Bell Aircraft officials, he directed that seventy qualified technicians from the 58th Bombardment Wing be sent to help the contractor complete the planes at the plant. Also, thirty additional Bell workers were brought in from one of the firm's other facilities to expedite the work. These actions, Arnold was advised, would do the job and his staff indicated he had no reason to be concerned that the deployment schedule would not be met. Subsequently, on 1st March, he wired Wolfe and CBI theater commanders that the B-29s would begin departing their Kansas bases on the 10th.

However, when he and an assistant, Major-General B E Meyer, arrived at Salina the afternoon of 9th March to watch the first departures, he was appalled to find that the planes still were not ready to go. The modification program, he discovered, was in complete chaos and, in his words, 'void of organization, management, and leadership.' There was no agency coordinating the work, which was being done not only at modification centres but at depots, sub-depots, and even in the B-29 squadrons. The situation was so chaotic that no one at Salina could tell him when or whether missing B-29 parts and items of equipment would arrive. A Technical Air Service Command officer, Colonel I W Stephenson, who witnessed Arnold's wrath, later described what happened: 'The General came in and . . . asked what was happening, who was running the show—and announced he was going to do it if no else was . . . and he wanted by [the following] morning a list of everything that was short; if it was in the factory; when it was going to be delivered . . .'

Arnold directed Meyers to remain at Salina to see that the list was completed and delivered to him at nearby Pratt field the next morning. As the angry Arnold flew off, Stephenson collected some aides and worked through the night of 9th-10th March to

Above: While bases for the B-29s were being constructed in India, airstrips in the vicinity of Chengtu, China, were being extended for use as forward bases with the aid of thousands of Chinese peasants. *Left:* At General Stilwell's request, Chiang Kai-shek agreed to improve a number of B-24 bases for use by B-29s. Immense gangs of Chinese laborers were employed for this task

prepare a report which, in chart form, showed the status of every B-29 on hand and the parts or items of equipment needed to put each plane into operating condition. When this paper was delivered to him, Arnold realized that not a single bomber was ready to depart. To recoup, he ordered an all-out crash effort, designating Meyers as his special Project Coordinator, with full authority to act in his name. The B-29 was assigned priority over all

other AAF aircraft programs. There followed a period of frenzied activity known in Air Force history as the 'Battle of Kansas' or the 'Kansas Blitz', an effort to complete and deploy 150 bombers to the CBI by mid-April.

Meyers chose a deputy and trouble shooter, Colonel C S Irvine, and charged him with responsibility for all matters pertaining to completing each plane and the proper functioning of all equipment up to the time it was delivered and accepted by 20th Bomber Command. Other knowledgeable technical and logistical personnel were brought in to help, among them Major Thomas Gerrity, to whom fell much of the actual work of expediting the modifications. It soon became evident to these men that the job could not be done with available, untrained personnel, mostly enlisted men and civilian workers. In desperation, they turned for assistance to the plane's producers, in particular to Boeing, and asked the loan of experienced assembly line workers and production men—even if this slowed down airframe production. Boeing responded by detailing some of its personnel to join in the crash effort to get the bombers operational. Meanwhile, subcontractors were ordered to stop everything else until they could provide the missing installations and parts, which soon were flowing into the Kansas bases by planes, trains, and trucks.

Beginning in mid-March—in the teeth of a raging snowstorm—Boeing's supervisors, the airmen, and civilian technicians and workers began the final installations of the missing parts on the B-29s parked on the flight lines. Civilians brought in from warmer climates were fitted out in sheep-lined flying suits so the work could proceed around the clock. Many became ill-tempered and, on one occasion, workers from the south complained their wages were below those received by northerners and they threatened a walkout. After General Meyers appealed to their patriotism

and spoke of the importance of the project, they agreed to remain. Finally, in late March, the first B-29 was certified as complete, was turned over to 20th Bomber Command, and, took off for India. Other bombers were finished during the weeks that followed and a stream of planes—150 of them—departed the United States, all of them by 15th April.

The flight from Kansas to India—11,530 miles—included stops at Marrakech, Cairo, Karachi, and Calcutta. The longest segment was a twenty-seven hundred mile overwater flight between Gander Lake and Marrakesh. In India, General Wolfe, together with American and British officials and newsmen gathered on the Chakulia flight line on 30th March 1944 to welcome the first bomber but, to their disappointment, it failed to arrive that day or during the next two days. Finally, on the afternoon of 2nd April, the dignitaries who gathered at the airstrip finally spotted the silvery B-29 in the distance. The pilot was General Saunders, who swept over the field, circled, and landed while Army cameramen recorded the scene. The second bomber arrived on 6th April, having come in from a stop-over in Britain. It had been sent there as part of a cover plan aimed at persuading the Germans and Japanese that it was intended for use in the impending Allied invasion of Hitler's 'Fortress Europe.' While in Britain, the B-29 was inspected by General Dwight D Eisenhower, General Doolittle, and top British officials and was duly photographed by a high-flying German reconnaissance aircraft.

Deployment of the other B-29s continued but not without incidents.

Left: One of the first B-29s rolled off the Wichita assembly line in the autumn of 1943. Deficient from the combat readiness standpoint, they were flown to modification centers in Kansas
Below: An early B-29 finished in olive drab and grey, a Bell-built example, after a crash landing near Karachi

On 13th April one plane was destroyed in a crash at Marrakesh but the crew escaped unharmed. On 15th April a second bomber crashed at Cairo; it was later repaired. The week that followed, however, turned out to be the worst in the entire history of B-29 oversea deployment. On two separate days, five bombers with overheated engines crashed near Karachi. Two were completely demolished and five crewmen were killed. Following these accidents, all B-29s were grounded while Wolfe initiated an investigation. He later attributed the engine failures to the generally high temperatures in the subcontinent, where ground temperatures frequently reached 115 degrees Fahrenheit or higher, and also to crew inexperience in operating with heavy loads. He wrote to Arnold that it was 'imperative that improved engine cooling be obtained immediately.'

In the United States, the problem was studied by engineering experts from Wright Field and the National Advisory Committee of Aeronautics. After conducting trial runs and test flights, they determined that the R-3350 engine was overheating primarily around the exhaust valves on the rear row of cylinders, causing complete engine failure. To correct this deficiency, fourteen new engine baffles were designed so that a blast of cooling air was directed on the rear exhaust valves. In addition, the top cowl flaps on each engine, which were originally fixed, were made operable from the cockpit and they also were shortened approximately three inches. A third major change was installation of crossover tubes from the intake to the exhaust port of the five top cylinders on both the front and rear rows. This provided a better flow of oil to the valves, which had been overheating. While this engine cooling project got under way, the flights of the B-29s to the theater were resumed. By 8th May, 148 had reached Marrakesh and 130 had arrived at their home bases in India.

The first
B-29 strike
against Japan

During the halt in the movement of the bombers to India, Generals Wolfe and Saunders on 24th April 1944 flew the first two B-29s over the Hump to Chengtu, a distance of more than 1,000 miles. Saunders arrived first at the Kwanghan airstrip, where Chennault together with Chinese officials and some 75,000 peasants who were still working on parts of the field welcomed the bomber and its crew. On 26th April two more B-29s made the trip and one of them ran into some Japanese fighters. The plane, piloted by Major Charles E Hanson, was sighted by twelve Japanese Oscars (Ki-43s) flying 2,000 feet below him. Six of the enemy fighters broke formation and began a climb which brought them close to the B-29 but out of range of its guns. The Japanese positioned themselves on each side of Hanson's bomber in lines of three astern, while they studied the phenomenon for some ten minutes.

They may well have reacted to the sight of the huge plane as did several other Japanese fighter pilots, Yasuo Kuwahara and Saburo Sakai, who described the B-29s in their postwar writings as 'stupendous giants' or 'tremendous bulls' Having gotten an eyeful, the enemy pilots reassembled in a loose, semi-circular formation and the lead plane launched an attack from below between four and five o'clock, which the pilot pressed to 400 yards before he turned off into a dive. During this first pass, the B-29 was hit and its left gunner slightly wounded. At this critical juncture, the bomber's defensive armament—through crew error or inexperience—went awry. The 50 caliber tail guns and three of the four upper guns jammed. The latter remained inoperative during the entire action. The 20mm cannon in the tail also remained silent through a crewman's failure to wind the spring loading mechanism. After the first damaging attack, the Oscars made two more single plane passes but they missed each time. As the fourth fighter came in from below at five to five-thirty o'clock, the tail gunner caught it with several bursts from his cleared 50 caliber guns, the Oscar began to smoke, broke away into a dive, and was not seen again.

At the start of the air action, Hanson altered course several times to give his gunners better targets. After his guns jammed, he put the ship into a gradual climb to 18,800 feet altitude, at which point the Oscars—having made eight more ineffective passes—broke off the attack. In all, the B-29 fired 400 rounds and suffered only light damage. Despite cabin bullet punctures, the pilot was able to maintain pressure by increasing the airflow from the engines. All Bomber

Oscars – the Nakajima Ki-43 Hayabusa of the Japanese Army, were the first Japanese fighters to encounter the B-29, on 26th April 1944. The picture shows the most widely used model at that time – the Ki-43-II KAI

61

Command crews greeted the news of this first combat by the B-29 not only with intense interest but satisfaction. The new bomber had been challenged, had been hit, and had flown on, and an enemy plane had probably been shot down. It seemed a good omen for the future.

Wolfe's staff, meanwhile, was settling in at Command headquarters at Kharagpur. It quickly discovered that American and Allied officials in India and China were not especially enthusiastic about the presence of the B-29s. The undertone of hostility had several sources. One was that the B-29s were considered an additional burden in a theater which, because Europe had priority, was receiving minimal logistic support. Another was that the bombers were not under the operational control of theater commanders. Concerning the first problem, AAF planners had originally argued that the B-29s would be self-sufficient. That is, with the help of transports assigned to the Command, they would

Above: **Numerically the most important fighter of the Japanese Army Air Force, the Oscar was encountered by the B-29 virtually everywhere that fighters opposed the bomber. Part of a Fighter Sentai operating the Ki-43-IIb version** *Right:* **A Ki-43-II Hayabusa at Kamiri, on the island of Noemfoor, photographed seconds before a 5th Air Force parachute bomb blasted it to extinction on 21st May, 1944**

be able to carry their own aviation gasoline, bombs, and other supplies to the China base to begin the strikes against Japan. It soon became evident that the concept was fallacious, that the B-29s could not airlift sufficient supplies to China to launch an early strike. Wolfe was forced to seek help from the theater's airlift organization, the Air Transport Command, which reduced the precious tonnage available to other commands.

Concerning the various commanders, both those in China and India believed that they should have

control of the bombers. As early as January 1944 Chennault wrote directly to the President asking that the B-29s be assigned to his command. In a separate letter to Arnold on the same day, 26th January, he argued that 'the commander of the air forces in China must be given complete command and control of all such air forces and supporting services as are based in or are operating from China.' In India, Lord Louis Mountbatten, Supreme Allied Commander, Southeast Asia, also wanted control of the B-29s to support his operations in the Burma-India area. While he accepted the decision that the B-29s were to be used primarily 'against Tokyo', he remarked to Wolfe that he should hope to see them employed in Southeast Asia which, he said with humor, would be 'the only rental we shall charge you for use of the theater.' Also, in the Southwest Pacific, General Douglas MacArthur sought the assignment of the B-29s to his command.

To help clarify command relationships, Washington officials decided to create a new B-29 air force which would be responsible directly to the Joint Chiefs of Staff. General Marshall later explained why. He said that:

'The power of these new bombers is so great that the Joint Chiefs of Staff felt it would be uneconomical to confine [them] . ... to a single theater. These bombers, therefore, will remain under the centralized control of the Joint Chiefs of Staff with a single commander, General Arnold, acting as their agent in directing their bombing operations throughout the world. The planes will be treated as major task forces in the same manner as naval task forces are directed against specific objectives.'

On 10th April the JCS issued a formal 'charter' for a new strategic Army Air Force – the Twentieth – operating directly under its control,

with Arnold serving as commander and its executive agent. Under terms of this charter, theater or area commanders were required to prepare suitable B-29 bases and to defend them, and to provide some logistical support. The Joint Chiefs, however, did allow for theater or area commanders to call upon the bombers whenever a special strategic or tactical emergency demanded. Both the US commander in China and the commander-in-chief of the Pacific Ocean Area later did so.

The Twentieth Air Force was formally, and secretly, activated in Washington on 4th April. Arnold requested his staff to perform its normal role for the Twentieth as well as for the other Army Air Forces but the primary plans and operations

Curtiss C-46 Commando flying the 'Hump', 1944

staff of the new organization consisted of a group of deputies headed by Brigadier-General H S Hansell, Jr, a key Arnold aide and chief of staff of the new air force. Hansell, a strong advocate of high altitude, precision bombing, had taught in the Air Corps Tactical School and served as a member of the War Department's Joint Strategic Committee. He had also served overseas as commanding general of the 1st Bombardment Wing and on the planning committee of the Supreme Allied Command. Later, he would head the 21st Bomber Command which began B-29 operations against Japan from the Marianas.

In India, meanwhile, Wolfe put a number of his B-29s to use as transports to carry essential supplies to China. The planes, which had an improvised fuel system with an off-loading manifold to permit them to be used temporarily as tankers, were stripped of all combat equipment except tail guns and radar. To help in this logistical effort, the War Department also sent out some C-46s to serve on the Hump run. Still, during April 1944 the planes were unable to airlift more than 1,400 tons of supplies to the China bases. Wolfe soon realized he could not launch his first strike against Japan on 1st May as planned. Instead of the 660,000 gallons of gasoline needed for two large strikes, the Command had only 380,000 gallons in storage. In this emergency, he ordered more B-29s stripped for the airlift task and, with great effort, each bomber was soon hauling seven tons of aviation gasoline per trip. He hoped

to accumulate about 4,400 tons so that the Command could launch the first raid in June and a second in July.

At this juncture, the enemy attempted to block the impending strikes by mounting a massive ground offensive in April and May 1944 known as Operation *Ichi-go*. Imperial General Headquarters, in a directive to General Shunroku Hada, commander-in-chief of the expeditionary army in China, stated that his primary mission was: 'To forestall the bombing of the Japanese Homeland by American B-29s from bases at Kweilin and Liuchow.' Hada was assigned other important objectives, including securing the Kweilin-Liuchow area in anticipation of Allied counteroffensives from India and Yunnan province, restoration of the north-south transcontinental railway network so as to renew land communications with Japanese forces in the south, and the destruction of the Chinese Army and dissolution of Chiang Kai-shek's government.

Tokyo's effort to prevent the bombing of Japan had its origin in intelligence it had received as early as April 1943 that the United States was building a long-range bomber. Confirmation came from various sources, and could well have included the *New York Times* of 5th November 1943, which published a press association report quoting Arnold to the effect that the Army's most powerful aircraft was in production. The AAF commander described the B-29 as a new, heavily armoured and armed plane, which could fly 'extremely high' and which had a 'substantially greater range' than the B-17 or B-24. Two months later, in an official

report released to the public. Arnold predicted that the new bomber 'will see action in 1944.' Finally, to further undermine B-29 security, the newspapers reported on 17th January that the Joint Aircraft Committee had assigned the B-29 the official name of 'Superfortress', because it was 'a gigantic "Flying Fortress", the B-17 type'.

In any event, the Japanese concluded on the basis of early intelligence that the United States would begin bombing operations from Chinese bases, probably from the Fourteenth Air Force fields around Kweilin and Liuchow, in late 1943. When the expected raids failed to materialize, they revised their estimates to project US deployment of B-29s to China by April or May 1944.

Their judgment that the bombers would be located at Kweilin and Liuchow apparently was based on information brought in by Chinese collaborators. Indeed, Chennault had strongly recommended those Fourteenth Air Force sites, pointing out that the B-29s would be able to fly directly to Japan without having to pass over occupied China and would have Kobe, Osaka, and Toyko within bombing range. If they were based at Chengtu, on the other hand, they would have to fly over Japanese-occupied territory in Central and North China, would alert the enemy, and further would be limited in strikes to the southern island of Kyushu. Arnold was willing to enlarge some of the fields Chennault recommended, but felt 20th Bomber Command should use them 'only for refueling, en route to or returning from targets in Japan,' since they could not be certain the Chinese would be able to hold them against the Japanese. At Stilwell's request, Chiang Kai-shek agreed to improve a number of the B-24 fields for B-29 use and, by July 1944, construction had been completed at Kweilin, Li-Chia-Tsun, and Liuchow.

Fortunately, Washington planners had decided to base the B-29s around

Lord Louis Mountbatten (center, facing camera), Supreme Commander Allied Forces Southeast Asia, visits a 20th Bomber Command B-29 base in India Left to right: Brigadier-General Kenneth Wolfe, Lord Mountbatten and Major- General Wildman Lushington

Chengtu after receiving Stilwell's pessimistic assessment of China's ability to ward off the enemy. He stated he would need fifty first class Chinese divisions to defend the Kweilin-Liuchow bases against a Japanese ground offensive and they did not exist. The Japanese, perhaps, were not aware of the Chengtu activity – or underestimated the range of the B-29s – when Hada's army launched Operation *Ichi-go* on 19th April 1944. The offensive's initial phase involved a strike into Central China against Chinese forces in Honan, with the goal of capturing the portion of the Peking-Hankow railway not already under Japanese control. As this operation came to a successful conclusion, General Hada – having assembled at Hankow and Canton in great secrecy a 400,000-man army, the largest Japan had ever thrown into a single campaign during the entire war – launched his main attack on 26th May on two fronts – to the south and west.

The Chinese were unable to halt this powerful horde. Changsha fell first to the Japanese on 18th June. The Chinese retreated to Hengyang, where for forty-nine days they put up an heroic resistance with great support from Chennault's fighters and bombers. But, in the end, the Allied effort failed and on 8th August Hada's army entered Changsha. The Japanese then pushed off to the southeast to seize Ling-ling on 4th September and, in their final drive, captured the Kweilin and Liuchow fields on 10th and 11th November and Nanning on 24th November. Yet despite these great land victories, Operation *Ichi-Go* failed to achieve its primary goal. The reason, as Colonel Saburo Hayashi, a Japanese historian of the Pacific war, has pointed out, was because it could not prevent the 'bombings of Japan

General Douglas MacArthur views the results of the heavy bombardment that prepared the way for the invasion of Los Negros Island in the Admiralty Group

proper by China-based American aircraft.' Two months after Hada had launched his offensive, the 20th Bomber Command finally struck the Japanese mainland in the first raid since Doolittle's planes hit Tokyo in 1942.

As was noted above, during April and May Wolfe and his crews struggled to build up their stockpiles of gasoline, bombs, and other materials at Chengtu for the first mission. The Japanese offensive worsened his situation, since Stilwell felt it necessary to divert some of the Hump tonnage previously allotted to 20th Bomber Command to Chennault's Fourteenth Air Force. During the *Ichi-go* crisis, Chiang Kai-shek and Chennault requested that all existing B-29 stockpiles at Chengtu also be turned over to the Fourteenth Air Force. In response to Stilwell's query to Washington, Marshall on 7th June 1944 directed that no B-29 stocks in China be released 'without the express approval from the Joint Chiefs of Staff.' He said it was the Chiefs' view 'that the early bombing of Japan will have a far more beneficial effect on the situation in China than the long delay in such an operation which would be caused by the transfer of those stocks to Chennault.' This decision put even greater pressure on Wolfe to launch the B-29s. The previous day Arnold sent him an urgent message, advising that the JCS required an early aerial attack on Japan proper to help relieve Japanese pressure in China and to coordinate with American landings in the Marianas, set for mid-June.

This message arrived the day after the 20th Bomber Command completed its first shakedown mission against Bangkok, Thailand. Of ninety-eight bombers sent out on a daylight precision strike against enemy railway shops, only forty-eight of the planes unloaded by radar (because of low clouds and haze) from 17,000 to 27,200 feet. The damage caused was negligible. Many planes aborted during this mission because of mechanical problems, while others failed to reach the

target. During the brief time the B-29s were over Bangkok, Japanese fighters and flak batteries opened up but no bombers were lost in combat. On the return flight, however, several B-29s were forced to ditch into the Bay of Bengal. In all, 20th Bomber Command lost five B-29s and fifteen men on the shakedown mission, but Wolfe felt the crews had gained valuable experience.

As he evaluated his resources for the first strike against Japan, Wolfe concluded that he would be unable to get more than fifty bombers over the target. This was not enough for Arnold; he directed Wolfe to launch at least a seventy-five plane mission. To reach that goal, Wolfe cut down fuel consumption in the forward area, put the 312th Fighter Wing on tight rations, and on 13th June began staging his bombers over the Hump to China. On the 14th he had eighty-three B-29s on hand at the Chengtu bases. His target – selected by Washington – was Japan's Iron and Steel Works at Yawata on the island of Kyushu. Intelligence analysts estimated Yawata's annual production at 2,260,000 metric tons of rolled steel, twenty-four percent of Japan's total.

One of the first B-29s to reach India. Indian women are carrying rubble away from the new runway

China, however, detected the B-29s long before they reached Japan and homeland fighters and antiaircraft units were alerted. The first B-29 flew over Yawata a half-hour before midnight to find the city perfectly blacked out. As the other formations arrived, Japanese searchlights and flak batteries suddenly began probing the skies and six Superfortresses were hit, although the damage was minor. Japanese fighters were up and made at least sixteen passes, but scored no hits.

The bombardiers in thirty-two B-29s, unable to see the target, unloaded by radar while fifteen others tried visual bombing. In the great confusion, some crews saw explosions on the ground but no one could tell whether the steel plant had been hit. Twenty-one of the Superfortresses failed to bomb the primary target, seven attempted to hit other targets and six jettisoned their bombs because of mechanical failures. On the return to Chengtu, two B-29s crashed in China, killing all on board including a war correspondent. The only known combat loss occurred when one ship developed a smoking engine two hours away from its home field and made a forced landing at dawn behind Chinese lines. Nationalist soldiers ran up soon after and warned the crew that Japanese planes would be over momentarily. Some thirty minutes after landing – while the Americans tried to figure out how to save their plane – Japanese fighters and bombers swooped in over the horizon and, after several bombing and strafing runs, left the B-29 a smoking ruin. The crew, with two wounded and a newsman, took cover in nearby ditches and were later rescued. In all, 20th Bomber Command lost seven planes, including a B-29 reconnaissance aircraft, and fifty-five men on its first mission over Japan,

On the morning of 14th June, the Superfortress crews were briefed on the mission. Late that afternoon, seventy-five bombers – each carrying two tons of explosives – began taking off. Eight war correspondents and three photographers rode with them as passengers. Trouble began immediately. Seven B-29s were unable to get airborne and, of those that did, one crashed immediately and four others were forced back by mechanical difficulties. The other sixty-three continued on towards Yawata, hoping to surprise the Japanese. Enemy radar on an island off the coast of

Above: Some of the tens of thousands of Indian peasants still engaged in enlarging the airfields as the B-29s arrived. *Below:* The first B-29 to reach the China-Burma-India Theater of Operations touches down at its base in India. *Left:* Japanese troops watch shells from their artillery bursting on Chinese positions

A 20th Bomber Command B-29 crossing the 'Hump' en route to a target in Japan on 21st November 1944. Cloud obscures the mountainous terrain below

all but one due to operational problems.

On the return to base, a number of crewmen expressed their belief that they had caused extensive damage to the steel works. However, reconnaissance photographs taken three days later showed little evidence of it. But the indirect results of the attack were considerable. Although Radio Tokyo belittled the raid, praised the 'quick and effective interception by the Japanese defenses,' and claimed six B-29s were shot down and that all was well, a Tokyo newspaperman later wrote that the Yawata attack 'sent a ripple of apprehension throughout the main islands of Japan.' In Chungking the news was greeted with applause and satisfaction by the Chinese, and General Wolfe issued a statement declaring the strike was 'but the beginning of the organized destruction of the Japanese industrial empire.'

In Washington, the work of Congress was halted while the news was read to the members of the House and Senate, and banner headlines reporting the raid got equal billing with news of the Allied armies breaking out of the Normandy beaches. A statement issued in Arnold's name (he was then visiting the Normandy battlefields) declared that the initial strike by the Superfortresses was the start of 'truly global aerial warfare.' In the new B-29s, it said, America possessed 'a highly complicated and most deadly airplane, capable of delivery of the heaviest blows yet known through air power.' What the statement did not say was that aviation fuel stockpiles were so low in China that the B-29s would be unable to launch another raid for several more weeks. The sustained, heavy bombardment of Japan remained many months off.

The air campaign out of China

Two days after the first strike at Yawata, Twentieth Air Force headquarters directed Wolfe to prepare to send his B-29s against targets throughout the length and breadth of the Japanese Empire, including enemy steel plants in Manchuria and Kyushu and a major oil refinery in Sumatra. Through such widespread attacks, Washington hoped not only to put a serious dent into Tokyo's war-making capacity but also to ease Japanese pressure on the Chinese and distract attention from the American invasion of Saipan, scheduled for mid-June 1944. But 20th Bomber Command was in great logistical trouble. Only a few days after the Yawata raid, its supply of gasoline in China totalled only 5,000 gallons and it

appeared impossible for it to quickly rebuild its reserves for an all-out mission against any enemy target. But on his return to Washington from his European inspection, Arnold wanted action. On 27th June he ordered Wolfe to launch fifteen B-29s against Japan in early July, one hundred against a major Japanese steel plant at Anshan, Manchuria, between 20th-30th July, and fifty against the oil refinery at Palembang, Sumatra, in August. To Wolfe, this schedule seemed entirely unrealistic, and in his operational plan – forwarded to Washington – he advised that, in order to carry out his directive, he would require additional B-29s plus a flat guarantee of some of the Hump tonnage being flown by the Air Transport Command. Even then, he said, he would be unable to get more than fifty or sixty bombers over Anshan.

Wolfe's plan did not sit well with the AAF commander and, on 4th July, Arnold ordered him to return to the United States to take over the Materiel Command, a job which rated a second star. To succeed Wolfe, Arnold chose Major General Curtis E LeMay, who at the age of thirty-eight had won a reputation in the European theater as a tough B-17 group and division commander. In Arnold's view, Wolfe's operations were 'very amateurish' in comparison with LeMay's. This criticism was somewhat unfair, given the initial misconception by the AAF planners (including Wolfe) that the B-29 could support itself logistically, plus the fact that the bomber was still full of mechanical bugs.

Wolfe broke the news to his staff the next morning (6th July, local time) and, in the process of trying to give the surprised officers a pep talk, he shed some light on the impatience of

Superfortresses of the 21st Bomber Command's 73rd Bombardment Wing flying in formation during a familiarization flight over the Marianas shortly after their arrival at Saipan during October-November 1944

Arnold: 'We have learned a lot of things here. We are just barely able to crawl and they call on us to do the one-hundred-yard dash . . . When you tell General Arnold you can get fifty aircraft [over the target], he says, "Fine, now get a hundred." When you tell him you can do something in a week, he says, "Fine, do it tomorrow." [However] that is why we have the Air Force we have today . . .' Wolfe urged his staff to continue their important work, which was, he said, 'the service testing, organizing, and experimenting for the whole B-29 effort.'

A few hours later he departed aboard a B-24 for the United States, leaving General Saunders in charge of operations. The following day, Saunders launched the Command's third raid – a small diversionary strike by eighteen B-29s against targets on Kyushu. Fifteen bombers reached the Japanese island, dispersed as planned, and unloaded their bombs on military and industrial facilities at Sasebo, Nagasaki, Omura, and Yawata. They caused little damage and all returned safely to base, although eight Japanese fighters attempted to intercept them over China. On 8th July Washington ordered the Command to attack Anshan and Palembang. Saunders was specifically directed to hit the Anshan facility with one hundred Superfortresses in a precision, daylight strike. During the next two weeks the B-29s flew repeated fuel airlift missions from India to China and, by the end of July, had managed with the help of transport aircraft to accumulate 3,954 tons at their Chengtu bases. On D-Day, 9th July, Saunders had 107 tactical B-29s in China (two others were lost over the Hump), yet he found it impossible to get one hundred planes airborne. The morning of the launch, one group of bombers became mired down on one of the runways because of heavy rains (sixteen of these aircraft were later sent against alternate targets). Of the seventy-two B-29s that actually departed for Anshan,

one crashed immediately, killing eight crewmen. Eleven other bombers failed to reach the target because of mechanical problems and two of these crashed.

As a consequence, only sixty Superfortresses reached the Manchurian facility in clear weather and under ideal bombing conditions. They began their runs at an altitude of 25,000 feet and speeds of up to 212 miles per hour. Unfortunately, bombs from the first planes produced a thick pall of smoke which obscured the aiming points for the B-29s that followed. The damage to the Anshan steel works proved disappointing. Of the estimated 2,574,644 metric tons of coke output by the plant, intelligence analysts – on the basis of reconnaissance photos – concluded production had been cut about seven and one-half percent. During the strike, enemy antiaircraft batteries sent up heavy flak and fighter aircraft also attacked the bombers. One Superfortress was downed, but eight of its crewmen were able to bail out and, with the aid of Chinese guerillas, reached Chengtu many weeks later. The B-29 gunners claimed three enemy aircraft probably destroyed and four damaged.

The third major target in this series – the oil refinery at Palembang – was one the Combined Chiefs of Staff had recommended during the Cairo conference. They believed the destruction of this facility, which reportedly produced twenty-two percent of Japan's fuel oil and seventy-eight percent of its aviation gasoline, would put a severe crimp in the enemy's operations. To reach Palembang, however, 20th Bomber Command had to stage the planes through Royal

Brigadier-General Laverne G Saunders, a B-17 pilot who had led combat missions at Guadalcanal, was assigned responsibility for the B-29 aircrew training programme. He later flew one of the first two B-29s to cross the 'Hump' from India to Kwanghan airstrip, Chengtu

Operations by 20th US Bomber Command

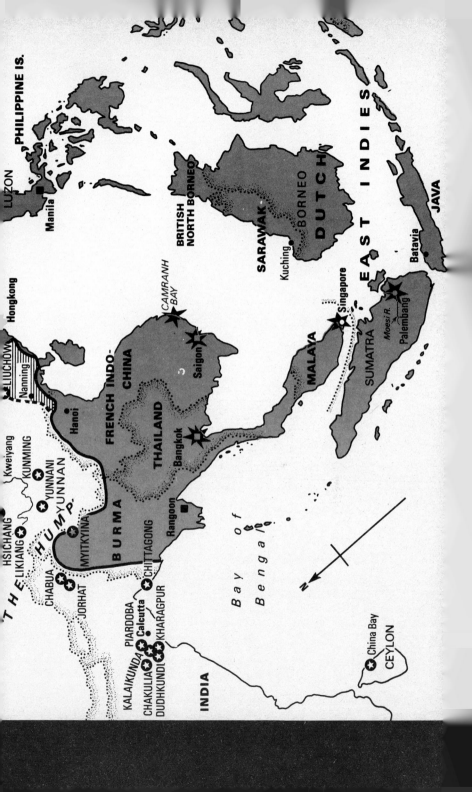

Top: Yawata burns for the third time.
Above: Bomb loading accident destroys a B-29 and damages another, 14th January 1945

Air Force bases in Ceylon and, even then, the distances were extreme – 1,900 miles. The Americans consulted with the British and initially proposed extending the runways of several existing airfields, but finally a decision was made to use a single field at China Bay, on the east coast of the island. Work on the China Bay strip was begun in the spring of 1944. As the facility neared completion, the Twentieth Air Force set 15th August as the deadline for conducting the operation. General Saunders selected D-Day for 10th August and began staging fifty-six bombers to the Ceylon base on the 9th. The attack on Palembang was planned as a night mission, with several B-29s assigned the separate task of laying mines in the Moesi river, through which all of the refinery's exports were shipped to Japan.

On 10th August, late in the afternoon, the first of the bombers sped down the China Bay runway and lifted off on what was a 3,800 mile round trip. One B-29 returned soon after takeoff with a leaky engine, was repaired, and went off again. Palembang was under a light cloud cover and showed no lights when thirty-one B-29s reached the area and unloaded their bombs by radar or visually through cloud patches. A dozen bombers failed to reach Palembang, while others bombed alternate targets. Eight planes also dropped sixteen mines into the Moesi. During the strike the B-29 crews sighted thirty-seven Japanese aircraft and, for the first time, encountered enemy ground-to-air rockets but they suffered no losses. One bomber, however, went down at sea on the return trip to Ceylon. Air-sea rescue units picked up its crew which lost only one man. The results of the Palembang raid, like the others, were poor. Even before photographic evidence of this was received, Saunders recommended to Washington – which eventually agreed – that they abandon Ceylon as a future staging base. Thus, no further B-29 raids were launched from China Bay and the only benefit from this single, inconclusive mission was that the bomber crews gained additional operational experience flying at extreme ranges.

The same day Palembang was struck, 20th Bomber Command sent a small force against the Nagasaki engine works on Kyushu. Twenty-nine B-29s – carrying a mixture of about three tons of incendiaries and fragmentation bombs in each plane – flew from their Chengtu bases, with twenty-four reaching the primary target. The city was hidden under a light cloud cover and blacked out when the bombers began unloading from high altitude. Once again, the results were disappointing with little damage done. The raid, however, was noteworthy in providing the Command its first official kill. An attacking enemy fighter was struck by a 20mm burst fired by one of the tail gunners and was seen crashing in flames.

On the basis of these early raids, the Japanese easily determined the types of targets the B-29s would hit and took vigorous steps to bolster their defenses around industrial and war production plants, especially in the Empire's Inner Zone – Manchuria, Korea, and the home islands. The results were seen in the reception given the Americans on 20th August 1944, when sixty-one B-29s struck again at Yawata in a daylight, high altitude raid. During the ensuing melee, the Japanese destroyed four Superfortresses. One was downed by a direct hit by flak and three by Japanese fighters, one of them by ramming. Eight other B-29s were damaged by flak. The Superfortress gunners claimed seventeen enemy aircraft destroyed, thirteen probably destroyed, and twelve damaged. After darkness fell, ten more B-29s returned to Yawata in a surprise, follow-up attack, but caused little damage.

The losses suffered by 20th Bomber Command on 20th August were considered heavy. Besides the four B-29s lost to enemy action, ten others were lost to operational causes and, by day's end, ninety-five crewmen were dead or missing. The men at Chengtu were later brought out of their gloom by news that one crew had bailed out east of Kharbarovsk, Siberia, and was safe, although interned by the Russians. At least three other B-29s would make forced landings in Soviet territory. During one of these, Soviet fighters fired on the Superfortress as it made its approach to the landing field. Puzzled by the hostility shown by the Russians, the crewmen – when they met the American Consul General and asked when they would be able to get their B-29 repaired and get back to the war – were told: 'You'll never see your plane again.' The confiscation of the B-29s by the Russians and their treatment of the crews 'like captured enemies, certainly not as allies,' rankled Arnold, who denounced it as 'inexcusable The reason apparently was Moscow's determination not to stir up the Japanese, with whom they had signed a Neutrality Pact in the spring of 1941. Eventually, the Russians – by surreptitiously moving the Americans at night – allowed the interned crews to 'escape' across the Iranian border several months later. As for the sequestered B-29s, the Soviets used them as models to manufacture a postwar duplicate for their own air force.

Chinese refuel by hand a B-29 after an emergency landing at Liangsham

General Saunders was preparing to launch another raid on the Anshan steel works when, on 29th August, LeMay arrived to take over command. He made no change in the plans for the strike, but went along as an observer in one of the 109 Superfortresses which took off for Manchuria on 8th September. Ninety-five reached the target area in good bombing weather and began their runs between 24,000 and 28,000 feet. In about an hour's time, they unloaded 206 tons of explosives on the Anshan works. Enemy fighter opposition was heavy and forty-eight Superfortresses were intercepted over the target.

However, the Japanese pilots seemed less aggressive and skilful than those encountered over Japan and B-29 gunners claimed eight enemy planes shot down, nine probables, and ten damaged. Four bombers were lost, three to operational causes and one to enemy planes which destroyed it on the ground after it made a forced landing. The crew of one missing plane, which crashed, later walked back to base having lost only one man. LeMay's bomber was hit by flak but pressurization was maintained and it made a safe return. Reconnaissance photos showed the bombs had caused considerable damage to Anshan. The Command's analysts estimated the facility's coke production had been cut by more than

thirty-five percent. The raid was considered the most successful launched to date.

Belatedly, in the early morning hours of 9th September 1944, the Japanese finally lashed out at the Chengtu bases. Enemy bombers – apparently guided to the scene by fires and flares set nearby by Chinese collaborators – swept over the airfield at Hsinching. In four quick passes they dropped a number of high explosives and fragmentation bombs, causing minor damage to one Superfortress and a transport plane. LeMay subsequently ordered a 'flare-observer system' be set up around the bases to provide some early warning in the future.

The 8th September raid was an auspicious start for the LeMay regime. One of his first actions following his arrival was to establish a 'Lead Crew' school at Dudhkundi and to require each bombardment group to send six crews to undergo special training. Its purpose was to provide lead crews, upon which others in the formations would follow. The eleven-day course was taught by the command's staff and specialists brought out to the theater. LeMay also did away with the existing four-plane diamond formation, substituting in its place a twelve-plane formation similar to the one he had used over Germany. In addition, since he intended to fly mostly daylight raids, he set up a special training course for his bombardiers and radar operators to govern the final bomb run. The decision as to which man would control the plane during the critical seconds before bombs away would be determined primarily by weather and visibility over the target.

The Command's next mission – its ninth – was run on 26th September, again to Anshan. The entire target area, however, was weathered in when the Superfortresses reached the scene and seventy-two B-29s – making their runs in the new twelve-plane formations – dropped by radar from 21,000 to 26,000 feet. They caused little damage to the facility. Although Japanese fighters rose to challenge the bombers and made some 248 passes, only nine B-29s were hit, one seriously, and there were no losses on the mission. The Superfortress gunners claimed eleven enemy planes destroyed, nine probables, and thirty-one damaged. That night, at Chengtu, the Command was alerted by a Chinese warning net that Japanese bombers had left Hankow fields in three waves heading west. The enemy force was plotted all the way in but, despite the advance warning, it was able to cause serious damage. Three strings of bombs damaged five Superfortresses and cut a communication line. A P-47 fighter, although airborne at the time, was unable to make contact. To beef up the defense against these strikes, LeMay requisitioned additional fighter aircraft and an antiaircraft unit. In all, the Japanese would send a total of forty-three planes on ten raids against the Chengtu bases, but they had little effect on B-29 operations.

It soon became evident that LeMay's improvements – and a subsequent Bomber Command reorganization which, among other things, did away with doubly trained crews and took the job of maintaining the planes away from the crews and assigned it to the more traditional maintenance units – did not get at the basic problem. That is, supplies still had to be flown over the Hump more than one thousand miles to the Chengtu bases. LeMay found, as had Wolfe before him, that the greatest flying effort of the Command was expended, as he later put it, 'in bringing in gas to those Chengtu strips.' He would conclude there could be 'no sustained and intensive effort by any bombers' required 'to feed their own fuel to themselves.' But, of course, the fact remained that for much of 1944, if Japan were to be bombed at all, it had to be from Chinese bases. Not until a new B-29 base was carved out in the coral rock of the Marianas in the summer and fall of 1944 would the role of 20th Bomber Command decline in importance.

Meanwhile, it continued to fly several important and successful mis-

Left: A reconnaissance photo of Tachikawa's aircraft assembly complex at Okayama on southern Honshu taken after a B-29 attack on 14th October 1944. *Above:* seaplane hangars at the Japanese Navy's Omura base

sions during the last months of 1944. One of these involved a coordinated Navy-20th Bomber Command attack on Japanese facilities on Formosa. First, on 12th-13th October, Navy carrier planes struck Japanese warehouses and wharves on Formosa and the Pescadores. Then, on 14th October, Bomber Command sent 130 B-29s against an aircraft plant at Okayama, the principal air installation on the island. 104 B-29s dropped 650 tons of bombs on the target – the heaviest load carried up to that time – and added substantially to damage caused there earlier by Navy aircraft. On 16th and 17th October, the B-29s returned to Formosa, wreaked additional havoc on Okayama, and also attacked two airfields and Takao harbor.

On 25th October, the B-29s struck the Omura aircraft plant on Kyushu, previously the target of a single Superfortress attack on the night of 7th-8th July 1944. The ordnance carried by the B-29s on this mission included a mixture of 500-pound M-64 general purpose bombs and 500-pound M-76 incendiary bombs, at a ratio of two to one. Visibility at Omura was unlimited when the B-29s began their attack about ten o'clock in the morning, Kyushu time. Seven formations dropped 156 tons on the target, while Japanese fighters and flak batteries tried to break up the bombing runs. One B-29, damaged in the battle, later crashed in China. However, its crew, except for the flight engineer, bailed out successfully. A second bomber was hit by flak, while twelve others suffered damage from enemy aircraft fire. B-29 gunners claimed ten Japanese aircraft destroyed. Reconnaissance photos showed destruction of a number of plant buildings, including a foundry, storage structures, a large assembly building, and other facilities. Damage to the major engine manufacturing works, however, appeared superficial.

On a return run to Omura on 11th November, the B-29s were pummeled by the weather, a new and dangerous adversary. Two days before, a typhoon was discovered south of Japan and Bomber Command forecasters pre-

Known to B-29 crews as 'Frank', Nakajima's Ki-84 Hayate was probably the most effective Japanese Army fighter encountered in large numbers. *Left:* Hayate of the 104th Fighter Sentai at Anzan, Manchuria. *Below left:* Hayates of the 52nd Fighter Sentai operating in the Philippines

dicted it would move in a direction south-east of the target. On the night of the 10th, with the Superfortresses airborne and heading for Kyushu, LeMay's weathermen belatedly decided that the typhoon would affect the target area and suggested a change. Via radio the ninety-six airborne B-29s were ordered to shift the weight of their attack to the last resort target at Nanking, China. However, twenty-nine bombers did not get the message and unloaded at Omura. But only five were able to bomb in formation because of severe turbulence, which threatened at times to tear the wings from the aircraft. Most of the other bombers hit at Nanking, as ordered, or other targets of opportunity.

The Nanking bombing produced substantial damage. According to a press service release out of Chinese Communist head-quarters in Yenan (based on a ground observer's report), the bombs hit railway tracks, an electric power station, the Japanese barracks, the puppet police station, and other buildings. Areas on both banks of the Yangtze were scorched, the entire Japanese Army barracks in the Tiger Bridge area was destroyed, as was the ticket office and waiting room of the Pukow railway station. One hundred enemy troops caught aboard a train at the station were reportedly killed. According to the Yenan report, so severe was the bombing that passenger trains from Shanghai to Nanking and from Nanking to Peking ceased to function on the 11th and 12th of November. Post-strike reconnaissance photos confirmed the destruction of three barrack-type buildings and a 'multiple-type' build-

Another potent interceptor met with by the B-29s was the barrel-like 'Jack', or Mitsubishi Raiden as it was known to the Japanese Navy. Largely confined to the defence of the home islands, the Raiden is seen here in its most extensively used form, the J2M3, that above being an example captured and flight tested at Clark Field

Awaiting the next mission.
Impressive row of 20th Bomber
Command B-29s at their base in
India

ing south of the railway station and,
to the north, the levelling of five
dormitory-type bays, a long warehouse, eight or ten miscellaneous
buildings, about fifty hutments, and
a passenger-loading platform, which
took a direct hit.

On 21st November – three days before Tokyo was finally struck by B-29s
based in the Marianas – the Command returned to Omura. On this
occasion, both the weather and enemy
fighters made life difficult for the
Americans and six B-29s were lost to
enemy action – the largest number up
to that time. 109 bombers took off on
the mission, but one immediately
crashed at Pengshan, killing all but
one crewman. Because of heavy clouds

over Omura, the crews had difficulty
seeing the target and most of the
bombers unloaded by radar. The
Japanese reacted strongly on this
occasion, sending aloft the Ki-84, a
more advanced, high speed fighter
(Allied code name, 'Frank'), which had
a speed of nearly 400 miles per hour at
21,300 feet. In addition, an advanced
version of the Japanese Navy's J2M1-5
interceptor (code name, 'Jack') made
an appearance. The Japanese had
incorporated an improved power plant
in this plane, enabling it to climb to
26,000 feet in under ten minutes.

All told, during the Omura raid
Japanese fighter pilots made more
than 300 passes at the B-29s. They shot
one down over the city and badly
damaged a second, which was unable
to make its base in China, crashing
thirty miles short. A third B-29, its
controls damaged by enemy fire,
managed to reach a friendly field at

Ankang but during the landing crash-ed into a parked Superfortress. Both were destroyed. Two other bombers also cracked up in China and two more were reported missing (one of these landed in the Soviet Union). In all, taking into account the one plane which crashed en route from India to China and the one at Pengshan, the 21st November raid cost 20th Bomber Command ten aircraft – of which six were lost to enemy fighter opposition, directly or indirectly – and fifty-three crewmen, dead, wounded, or missing. The B-29 gunners, however, claimed twenty-seven enemy planes destroyed, nineteen probables, and twenty-four damaged.

The growing aggressiveness of the Japanese Air Force was seen again during a ninety-plane mission against the Manchurian Aircraft Company at Mukden on 7th December 1944. During this Superfortress strike, some eighty-five Japanese fighters made 247 attacks on the bombers. One B-29, severely hit by shell fire, was aban-doned by its crew. Japanese planes rammed two others while a third, apparently accidently struck by an enemy aircraft in its number one propeller, managed to fly all the way back to its base, although the plane that hit it was destroyed. The Mukden air action also featured a Japanese tactic new to 20th Bomber Command, air-to-air bombing. Enemy fighters – flying directly toward the B-29s from above – dropped phosphorus bombs containing time fuses set to produce air bursts immediately in the path of the American planes. At Mukden at least one B-29 was damaged in this manner. The tactic was later used extensively by the Japanese during their desperate defense of the home islands in the face of accelerating B-29 attacks.

The Hankow raid and the end of China operations

In December 1944 the B-29 crews flew one of their most important missions against the city of Hankow on the Yangtze river, captured by the Japanese in 1938 and built into a huge military supply center. The significance of the raid was the influence it would have on B-29 operations launched from the Marianas. The target was chosen by Chennault. In June 1944, as the enemy's *Ichi-go* offensive picked up momentum, he had urged 20th Bomber Command to divert one hundred B-29s to destroy Hankow's port facilities with incendiaries and thus 'undermine the enemy's entire effort in East China.' However, Wolfe and Saunders – with the support of General Arnold – were determined the Superfortresses would not end up in 'a theater air force.' They believed the B-29 had 'a war of its own to fight' in the enemy's heartland and should not be diverted against tactical targets. They agreed only to list Hankow as a secondary or alternate target and the city was struck

on two occasions by several B-29s which, for various reasons, were unable to hit their primary targets.

The Command's opposition to theater missions remained unchanged even after the arrival in China of Lieutenant - General Albert C Wedemeyer, who replaced Stilwell in the fall of 1944. Soon after he reached Chungking on 31st October to take charge of the newly-formed China theater (the India-Burma area was made a separate theater), Wedemeyer ordered LeMay to run the Hankow mission as requested by Chennault. LeMay demurred, citing his old directives, and it required a JCS order confirming Wedemeyer's authority to get 20th Bomber Command to respond. After receiving the JCS directive, LeMay flew to Kunming to consult with Chennault on a strike plan which would involve the participation not only of the B-29s but also of Fourteenth Air Force B-24s, B-25s, and P-51s. Later he flew to Chungking to review the plan with Wedemeyer.

During their Kunming meeting, the two air generals disagreed for a time over tactics. Chennault urged LeMay to use only incendiaries on the mission and to drop them from below 20,000 feet to ensure accuracy. The latter suggestion, however, was contrary to existing Twentieth Air Force doctrine, which required high altitude bombing. (Most of the B-29 strikes up to that time had been from above 25,000 feet.) But after listening to Chennault's arguments, LeMay agreed to deviate from existing doctrine for the Hankow mission. The 20th's commander had shown similar flexibility in Europe, where he had ignored conventional bombing wisdom and saw the results in a higher percentage of enemy targets hit. When he first arrived overseas, most B-17 squadrons flying to the continent took evasive action to avoid German flak and, as a consequence, rarely hit their targets. LeMay devised a tight combat formation for his bombers and ordered the pilots to make their runs

Major-General Albert C Wedemeyer (right), at whose insistence 20th Bomber Command B-29s participated in the Hankow attack, is seen with Chinese peasants during an inspection tour

straight into the targets, despite enemy flak. This tactic greatly increased the number of hits and was eventually adopted by the Eighth Bomber Command. Now, at Kunming, he agreed to drop the B-29s to a lower altitude – to 18,000 to 21,000 feet – and also to load up four out of each five bombers with incendiaries, with each fifth plane carrying demolition bombs. The strike was set for 18th December.

The morning of the mission, however, the plan went slightly awry. About six hours before takeoff, Chennault requested LeMay's headquarters to launch the B-29s forty-five minutes earlier than previously scheduled. For some reason, the information failed to reach three of the four bombardment groups, with the result that the planes that should have

A section of Hankow waterfront after the attack of 18th December 1944

bombed first arrived among the last formations. The carefully laid sequence of attack thus miscarried, and within a short time after the first wave of planes dropped on the target, the city was blanketed by thick, black smoke. The six elements that followed had difficulty finding their aiming points and unloaded in the general area. The last bombs were dropped sixty minutes after the strike began.

In all, eighty-four B-29s unloaded more than 500 tons of incediaries on the city. They were followed by the bombers and fighters of the Fourteenth Air Force, which added to the destruction. Huge fires were set along the entire length of Hankow's three mile long Yangzte waterfront and burned for three days, gutting the docks, warehouse areas, and adjacent sectiors of the city. Chennault later described the attack as 'the first mass fire-bomb raid' by the Superfortresses and claimed that its success so impressed LeMay that the B-29 commander adopted the technique when he took over air operations in the Marianas. In his memoirs, LeMay acknowledges the influence of the Hankow raid on his thinking. Everything, he recalled, 'burned like crazy' and he remembered there was 'a vast similarity' between the type of construction in Hankow and that in Japan.

The vulnerability of Japan's cities to aerial attack had been carefully noted as early as 1924 by Billy Mitchell, during his tour of the Far East. In his report to the War Department in which he summed up his observations, Mitchell described Japan's cities as 'congested and easily located, their structures paper and wood or other inflammable substitutes.' But it was Chennault who was the first American general who actually witnessed the effectiveness of incendiary bombing of Oriental cities. For several years in the late 1930s he had watched the Japanese fire-bomb Chinese cities and towns with gruesome results, and as early as 1940 he wrote to Arnold, urging him to develop five-pound fire bombs for use against Japan. This suggestion was badly timed. That is to say, President Roosevelt had repeatedly denounced the bombing of civilians in undefended cities. Thus, in his reply to Chennault, Arnold reminded him that the use 'of incendiaries against cities was contrary to our national policy of attacking only military objectives' and that the Air Force was 'committed to a strategy of high-altitude precision bombing...'

Washington's attitude, however, began to soften after the Luftwaffe – defeated in the Battle of Britain – resorted to indiscriminate incendiary attacks on London and other English towns. During these raids, the Germans dropped two-pound cylinders of magnesium, later modified with an explosive charge to prevent British firefighters from scattering them. In the spring of 1941, during a visit to London, Arnold was provided some of these bombs and several British models. When he returned to the United States, he requested Dr Vannevar Bush, who headed America's wartime scientific research efforts, to study ways to improve such fire bombs for use both by the AAF and the Royal Air Force. Meanwhile, the Army's Chemical Warfare Service and Ordnance Department – after studying Arnold samples – put into production a series of small, modified

incendiaries – the AN-50, AN-52, and AN-54. The last incendiary, built with a steel case because magnesium was in short supply and packed into 500-pound clusters, was dropped on Tokyo by Doolittle's raiders in April 1942.

Despite his protests against the bombing of undefended cities, Roosevelt appears after Pearl Harbor to have found definite merit in Churchill's suggestion, made to him in a paper entitled 'Notes on the Pacific', which dealt with strategy. In this paper, dated 20th December 1941, Churchill foresaw that superior Allied battle fleets and seaborne air power would lead to the acquisition or regaining of 'various island bases' which, he said, could then be used to attack the Japanese homeland. 'The burning of Japanese cities by incendiary bombs,' Churchill wrote, 'will bring home in a most effective way to the people of Japan the dangers of the course to which they have committed themselves . . .'

The general notion of striking back at Japan was one which Chennault and the Chinese had wanted to implement for many years and which, as we have seen, Roosevelt approved in December 1940. Several years later, when the President's special emissary, Wendell L Wilkie, visited China, Chennault submitted a lengthy letter to him on 6th October 1942, in which he outlined his plan to destroy the principal centers of Japan from bases in China. If provided the necessary resources, Chennault promised his bombers could 'burn up Japan's two main industrial areas – Tokyo and the Kobe, Osaka, Nagoya triangle . . .' Although most of the top AAF leadership was still committed to the doctrine of high altitude precision bombing of military targets, they did authorize studies which looked into the entire question of incendiary attacks.

Meanwhile, a group of scientists in Division 11 of the National Defense Research Committee by 1942 had invented a much-improved incen-

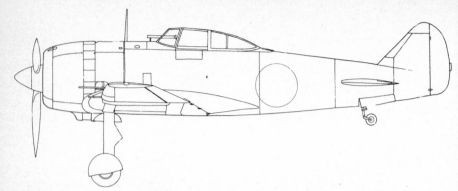

'Tojo': The Nakajima Ki-44 Shoki (Demon) was one of the major opponents of the B-29 over Japan's home islands and elsewhere. It entered service with the Japanese Army Air Force late in 1942, and was the first Japanese fighter to emphasize speed and climb rather than maneuverability. High-speed snap rolls, spins and stalls were restricted, but climb and dive capabilities were outstanding. The following relate to the Ki-44-IIb model of 1943. *Power Plant:* Nakajima Ha-109 of 1,520hp for take-off. *Armament:* Four 12.7mm Type 1 machine guns. *Maximum speed:* 376mph at 17,060 ft. *Climb:* 4 min 17 sec to 16,400ft, 9 min 37 sec to 26,250ft. *Service ceiling:* 36,745ft. *Weight empty:* 4,643 lb. *Weight loaded:* (Normal) 6,107 lb. *Span:* 31ft. 0in. *Length:* 28ft. 9¾in.

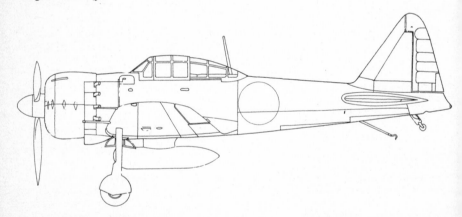

'Zeke': The Mitsubishi A6M Reisen (Zero Fighter) appeared ubiquitous in the opening phases of the Pacific conflict, but by the time it participated in the desperate attempts to ward off the Marianas-based B-29s it was outmoded. Possessing remarkable maneuverability, this Japanese Navy fighter acquired a near-legendary reputation. Numerous models were introduced into service, one of the later variants being the A6M8 to which the following details apply: *Power Plant:* Mitsubishi MK8P Kinsei 62 of 1,560hp for take-off. *Armament:* Two 20mm Type 99 cannon and two 13.2mm Type 3 machine guns. *Maximum speed:* 356mph at 19,685ft. *Climb:* 6 min 50 sec to 19,685ft. *Service ceiling:* 37,070ft. *Weight empty:* 4,740 lb. *Weight loaded:* (Normal) 6,945 lb. *Span:* 36ft. 1in. *Length:* 30ft. 3in.

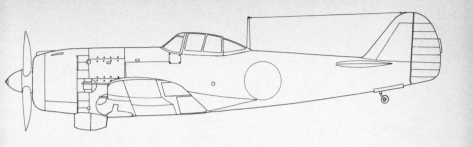

'Frank' The Nakajima Ki-84 Hayate (Gale) is generally considered to have been the best Japanese fighter to have operated in substantial numbers in WW II. Serving with the Army, it was fast, highly-maneuverable and relatively well armed. In short a formidable opponent by any standard. The most common version was the Ki-84-Ia. *Power Plant:* Nakajima Ha-45 of 1,900hp for take-off. *Armament:* Two 20mm. Ho-5 cannon and two 12.7mm Ho-103 machine guns. *Maximum speed:* 388mph at 19,680ft. *Climb:* 5 min 54 sec to 16,400ft., 11 min 40 sec to 26,240ft. *Service Ceiling:* 34,450ft. *Weight empty:* 5,864 lb. *Weight loaded:* (Normal) 7,965 lb. *Span:* 36ft. 10$\frac{1}{4}$in. *Length:* 32ft. 6$\frac{1}{2}$in.

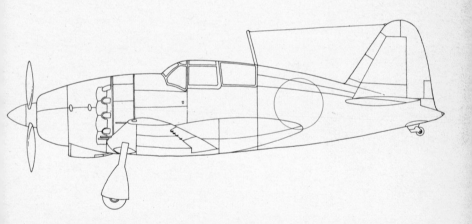

'Jack': The Mitsubishi J2M Raiden (Thunderbolt) was the Japanese Navy's equivalent of the Army's Ki-44 Shoki in that accent was placed on speed and climb rather than maneuverability. It suffered a string of teething troubles, some of which were never entirely overcome, but JNAF pilots preferred it to all other available single-seaters for the bomber intercept role. The J2M3 model, to which the following figures apply, was built in largest numbers. *Power Plant:* Mitsubishi MK4R-A Kasei 23a of 1,820hp for take-off. *Armament:* Four 20mm Type 99 cannon. *Maximum speed:* 365mph at 17,390ft, 371mph at 19,360ft. *Climb:* 2 min 56 sec to 9,840ft, 5 min 40 sec to 19,685ft. *Service ceiling:* 38,385ft. *Weight empty:* 5,423 lb. *Weight loaded:* (Normal) 7,573 lb. *Span:* 35ft. 5$\frac{1}{4}$in. *Length:* 32ft. 7$\frac{3}{8}$in.

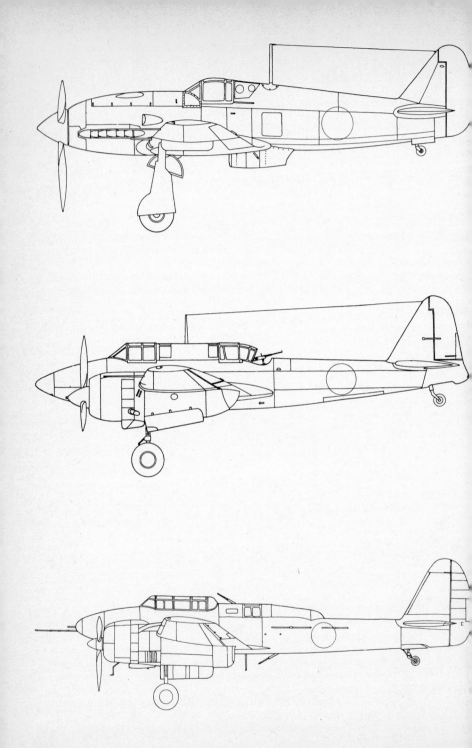

'Tony': The Kawasaki Ki-61 Hien (Swallow) was unique among Japanese Army service single-seat fighters in having a liquid-cooled engine. It entered service early in 1943 as the Ki-61-I and subsequently saw extensive service. Plagued with engine problems throughout its life, the Ki-61 was nevertheless at one time the most potent of the Japanese Army's fighters. The following details apply to the Ki-61-Ic. *Power Plant:* Kawasaki Ha-40 of 1,175hp for take-off. *Armament:* Two 20mm Ho-5 cannon and two 12.7mm Type 1 machine guns. *Maximum speed:* 348mph at 16,400ft., 366mph at 13,980ft. *Climb:* 7 min to 16,400ft. *Service ceiling:* 32,800ft. *Weight empty:* 5,798 lb. *Weight loaded:* (Normal) 7,650 lb. *Span:* 39ft. 4in. *Length:* 29ft. 4in.

'Nick': Kawasaki Ki-45 Toryu (Dragon Killer) took an active part in the defence of Japan against B-29 attacks, serving Japanese Army intercept elements in both day and night roles. The primary model encountered by the B-29 was the Ki-45 KAIc, and many fighters of this type were assigned to the nocturnal intercept mission when the B-29s switched to low-level night attacks. *Power Plant:* Two Mitsubishi Ha-102s of 1,080hp for take-off. *Armament:* One 37mm Ho-203 cannon and two obliquely-mounted 20mm Ho-5 cannon. *Maximum speed:* 335mph at 19,685ft. *Climb:* 7 min to 16,400ft. *Service ceiling:* 32,800ft. *Weight empty:* 8.818 lb. *Weight loaded:* (Normal) 12,125 lb. *Span:* 49ft. 3$\frac{1}{4}$in. *Length:* 36ft. 1in.

'Irving': Nakajima J1N Gekko (Moonlight) was evolved for the Japanese Navy as a long-range fighter primarily for the escort role. Rejected, it was redesigned as a fast reconnaissance aircraft but was adapted in 1943 for night fighting as the J1N1-C KAI illustrated here. This was fitted with a pair of 20mm cannon fixed to fire forward and upward and two similar weapons firing forward and downward. The definitive model, the J1N1-S, was built primarily for night fighting but was frequently encountered by B-29s during daylight attacks, and the following figures apply to this version. *Power Plant:* Two Nakajima NK1F Sakae 21/22s of 1,130hp for take-off. *Armament:* Four obliquely-mounted 20mm Type 99 cannon. *Maximum speed:* 315mph at 19,030ft., 305mph at 10,830ft. *Climb:* 5 min 1 sec to 9,840ft., 9 min 35 sec to 16,400ft. *Service ceiling:* 30,580ft. *Weight empty:* 10,697 lb. *Weight loaded:* (Normal) 15,983 lb. *Span:* 55ft. 8$\frac{1}{2}$in. *Length:* 39ft. 11$\frac{1}{2}$in.

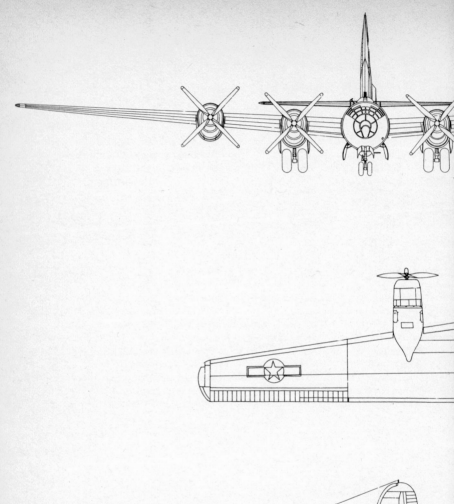

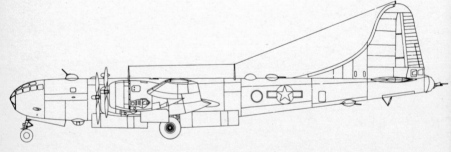

B-29 Superfortress: *Power Plant:* Four Wright R-3350-23s each rated at 2,200hp. *Armament:* Ten-twelve 0.5in. machine guns and one 20mm cannon for defence plus four 4,000 lb., eight 2,000 lb., 12-1,000 lb., 40-500 lb., 50-300 lb., or 80-100 lb. bombs. *Maximum speed:* 365mph at 25,000ft. *Long-range cruise:* 220mph. *Service ceiling:* 31,850ft. *Range:* 5,830 miles. *Weight empty:* 69,610 lb. *Weight loaded:* 105,000 lb. *Span:* 141ft. $2\frac{3}{4}$in. *Length:* 99ft.

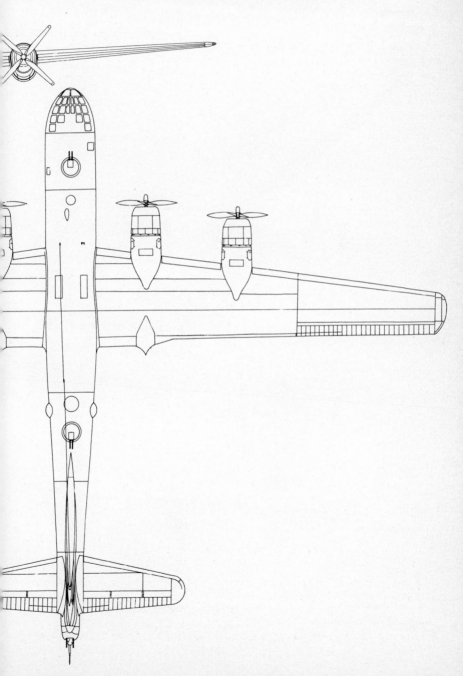

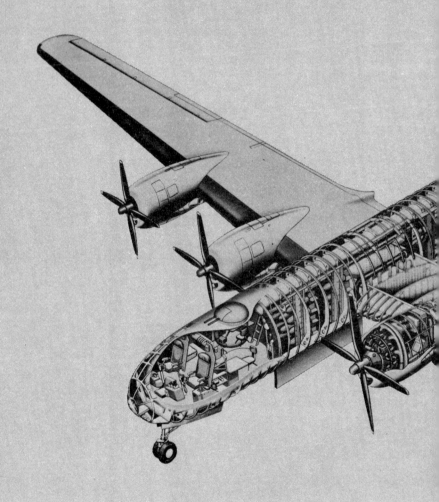

diary, consisting of a new material they called petroleum jelly or napalm. The material was first incorporated into the M-47, a 70-pound incendiary bomb developed by the Chemical Warfare Service. Later, it became the main ingredient of a six-pound bomb designated the M-69. Unlike other incendiaries, which burned where they fell, the M-69 contained a mechanism which threw out masses of napalm that stuck to walls and ceilings of buildings and burned fiercely. Another M-69 innovation was the use of cloth ribbons as stabilizers, instead of metal fins, to save weight and keep it from dropping too fast.

This napalm-filled bomb was put into production in November 1942. It was later tested against industrial-type buildings at Edgewood Arsenal, Maryland, a simulated Japanese village constructed at Eglin Field, Florida, and a small German-Japanese village constructed on the Dugway Proving Ground, Utah. Although the experiments demonstrated its superiority over other incendiary bombs, they also disclosed several weaknesses. The M-69 tended to wobble as it fell and was not always accurate. In addition, about twenty percent of the bombs dropped at Dugway were duds. The AAF considered the M-69, and all other existing incendiary bombs tested, as inadequate for combat operations.

Its view was best expressed by Brigadier General B W Chidlaw, Headquarters AAF, in a letter on 15th April 1943 to the Commanding General of Army Service Forces. Chidlaw declared that the fundamental basis of all projected AAF bombardment operations was 'precision bombing of specific military targets.' To permit effective use of incendiary bombs in those operations, he said, it was necessary that the bombs 'be of a type and design capable of meeting conditions of large industrial targets, and having ballistic properties permitting precision bombing, comparable to demolition bombs.' In response to this statement of policy, the Army's Ordnance Department initiated a project to develop a class of improved 'aimable' incendiary bombs.

Aimable incendiaries were desirable, but a major change in AAF tactics was forecast in the fall of 1944 by a group of scientists, who had studied the economic damage that might be done to Japan through the extensive use of such bombs. In their report to Dr Bush on 12th October, which he forwarded to the AAF, they made the following remarkable prediction:

'Advance estimates of force required and the damage to Japanese war potential expected from incendiary bombing of Japanese cities indicate that this mode of attack may be the golden opportunity of strategic bombardment in this war – and possibly one of the outstanding opportunities in all history to do the greatest damage to the enemy for a minimum of effort. Estimates of economic damage expected indicate that incendiary attack of Japanese cities may be at least five times as effective, ton for ton, as precision bombing of selected strategic targets as practiced in the European theater. However, the dry economic statistics, impressive as they may be, still do not take account of the further and unpredictable effect on the Japanese war effort of a national catastrophe of such magnitude – entirely unprecedented in history.'

It was this kind of projection, along with other studies, which led Twentieth Air Force planners to order test incendiary strikes against Japanese cities by 21st Bomber Command in the Marianas. The damage achieved by LeMay's and Chennault's strike at Hankow on 18th December 1944 seemed to bear out the scientists' forecast of the damage that could be done by fire-bombing the inflammable structures of Oriental cities.

These were matters for the future, however, and would not involve 20th Bomber Command, which was near the end of its operations in China. By

December 1944 it had become apparent to all concerned that the Marianas operations had undercut their original mission. An American Congressman, Rep. Mike J Mansfield, of Montana, after a visit to the B-29 bases in China that month, reported to the President in January 1945 that 'the feeling of the men at Chengtu is that the usefulness of the fields there is not worth the price in maintaining, now that the 21st Bomber Command has been activated on Saipan. The supply problem, vulnerability of the fields, and the distances involved, make it a difficult situation.'

Not only did the aircrews of the 20th want to get out of China, but Chennault and Chiang Kai-shek wanted them out to ease the supply situation. The US ambassador to China, Patrick J Hurley, supported their withdrawal request in a message to Washington in late October 1944. General Wedemeyer, in response to a JCS query, also recommended that 20th Bomber Command be removed as soon as possible. The JCS delayed its decision, since MacArthur had requested B-29 support for his Luzon landings, which took place on 9th January 1945. Three days after the operation began, Wedemeyer again urged removal of the B-29s. Finally, on 15th January, at Arnold's suggestion, the Joint Chiefs agreed.

In the meantime, to support MacArthur's operations, 20th Bomber Command flew a number of missions from Chengtu aimed at reducing Japanese air power. Three days before the troops hit the beaches at Lingayen Bay, twenty-eight B-29s attacked the Omura aircraft assembly and repair plant on Kyushu. On 9th January, in what was considered a direct support mission, forty-six bombers were sent against Japanese aircraft facilities at Kiirun, Formosa. The Command hit island targets again on the 14th, when fifty-four B-29s dropped about 300 tons of bombs on Kagu, causing substantial damage. Three days later seventy-nine B-29s returned to Formosa to hit enemy facilities at Shichiku. Even as this raid was under way, plans for evacuation of 20th Bomber Command from China – made weeks before – were implemented. By 28th January all personnel, planes, and equipment were removed to India, where the final phase of the 20th's combat operations began, this time under the overall command of Lord Mountbatten.

The Supreme Allied Commander, Southeast Asia, was assigned operational control of 20th Bomber Command for a number of months in early 1945. Mountbatten later wrote of the strategic bombers that 'they did excellent work' against targets beyond the range of other theater aircraft, 'particularly in long-range mine-laying which I specially called for, against such distant targets as Singapore, Saigon, and Camranh Bay.' Beginning on the night of 25th-26th January, the B-29s launched the first of this new series of strikes, which were continued through February and March. On two occasions the B-29s returned to their old China bases, from where they carried out minelaying missions to the Yangtze river. The Command's last mission – its forty-ninth – was an attack on Singapore's oil facilities on 29th March 1945.

In all, by the time 20th Bomber Command went out of business, its B-29s had flown 3,058 sorties from China and India and dropped 11,477 tons of bombs on enemy targets. It also had flown 3,405 transport sorties in support of the China-based missions. The results were not what was originally hoped for. Nevertheless, the B-29 operations from India and China had served the important purpose of shaking down the new bomber and the theater had served well 'as a great combat testing laboratory for the coming phase of strategic air power.' Most of the men and planes, beginning on 24th February, began redeploying to the Marianas to participate in that final phase of operations.

B-29 strikes from the Marianas

At the Trident conference in Washington in May 1943, Roosevelt, Churchill, and their military aides had accepted the proposition that military operations in and from China were essential to the ultimate defeat of Japan. During subsequent discussions of ways to land Allied forces on the Chinese mainland, Admiral Ernest J King, the US Chief of Naval Operations, proposed an American drive through the Central Pacific to include the seizure of the Marianas, some 1,500 miles south of Tokyo, which he considered the key to the western Pacific. No action was taken on King's proposal at the conference, however, nor at the August meeting of the Allied leaders at Quebec, where Arnold submitted the 'Air Plan for the Defeat of Japan'.

Since it had been assumed no Pacific islands would be in American hands within B-29 striking distance from Japan, Arnold recommended, as noted earlier, basing the bombers in China to begin the early bombing of the Japanese mainland. However, following the Quebec conference, AAF officials took another look at the possibility of also basing the B-29s in the Marianas, which they suddenly realized were well within the cruising range of the Superfortresses.

On 4th October 1943, at the urging of its AAF and Navy members the US Joint Planning Staff recommended that plans for accelerating the defeat of Japan 'place emphasis on the seizure of the Marianas at the earliest possible date, with the establishment of heavy bomber bases as the primary mission.' At Cairo in December 1943 the proposed operation was approved by the Combined Chiefs of Staff and by Roosevelt and Churchill. In their 2nd December 'Overall Plan for the Defeat of Japan,' the Combined Chiefs declared their ultimate goal was to seize bases 'from which we can conduct intensive air bombardment and establish a sea and air blockade against Japan, and from which to invade Japan proper if this should become necessary.' In addition to the Central Pacific drive, they endorsed operations on the jungle road to Tokyo along the New Guinea-Netherlands East Indies-Philippine route. Both drives were deemed mutually supporting but in case of conflict, they thought 'due weight should be given to the Central Pacific campaign, as it promised 'a more rapid advance toward Japan and her vital lines of communications.'

Not long after these decisions were made, instructions were sent to Admiral Chester W Nimitz, Commander-in-Chief of the US Pacific

Smoke billows up from an aircraft factory north of Tokyo. Photograph taken during a B-29 strike on 10th January 1945

Fleet, to prepare a plan of operations. This plan, as it took form, initially included an American invasion and seizure of some nine enemy-held islands – Kwajelein, Kavieng, Manus, Eniwetok, Mortlock, Truk, Saipan, Tinian, and Guam – beginning in January 1944 and running through November of that year. Second thoughts and changed conditions led to important revisions in the plan as time passed. Truk was bypassed, the Palaus were invaded ahead of schedule, and the Marianas operation also was moved up. Not surprisingly, MacArthur was strongly opposed to the Central Pacific strategy as adopted at Cairo. He believed that all forces should be concentrated under his command in the Southwest Pacific for a series of operations that would include recapture of the Philippines. Advocates of the two strategies debated the matter at high-level meetings in Hawaii and Washington. In March 1944, however, the Joint Chiefs of Staff reaffirmed the Central Pacific venture, with minor modifications, and set 15th June 1944 for the invasion of the Marianas.

The first objective was the island of Saipan, a little more than 1,500 miles from Tokyo, which the Japanese had built into a bristling fortress defended by 30,000 well dug-in troops. On 11th June the pre-invasion bombardment began, continued for four days, and was followed by the storming of the beaches by two Marine divisions. An Army division landed on the island on D-Day plus one to join the battle. The Japanese fought desperately to the bitter end, with the struggle highlighted by the war's biggest suicidal *Banzai* charge on the night of 6th-7th July. More than 3,000 enemy troops – issued instructions to kill ten Americans for each Japanese slain – charged the lines of the Army division and caused huge casualties before all of them were killed. By 9th July all organized resistance had ended. The Japanese lost 23,811 dead, the Americans, 3,426 killed and missing and

13,099 wounded. It was a costly victory but President Roosevelt considered the operation 'an outstanding success explaining in a letter to a friend on 20th July that it gave the United States a base within 'easy bombing range' of the industrial part of Japan. The same day he expressed this view, other American invasion forces landed on Guam and, on 23rd July, on Tinian. By 9th August they had wrested both islands from the Japanese.

News of the loss of Saipan – coupled with the start of the bombing of Kyushu by the China-based B-29s – came as a severe shock to the leaders of Japan. Prince Higashi-Kuni, a member of the Supreme War Council and Commander-in-Chief of Home Defense Headquarters in Tokyo, later testified that the Japanese government realized that the B-29 was an extraordinary airplane and that they lacked a means 'that we could use against such a weapon.' With B-29s based on Saipan, the vulnerability of Tokyo and much of Japan proper became apparent to the entire leadership. One immediate result of Saipan's fall was the resignation of Hideki Tojo, the Japanese Premier and former War Minister. He was succeeded by Premier Kuniaki Koiso; however, the Japanese military continued in firm control of the government and at once began making plans to attack the airfields on Saipan, which they realized would soon be built.

This construction work indeed began on 24th June. Even as the battle raged around them, aviation engineers began laying out the first of five great airfields which were to be eventually established on Saipan, Tinian, and Guam. First to become operational was a runway designated as Isley Field, built on the site of an old Japa-

A badly-damaged B-29 that didn't quite make its base on Saipan on 27th February 1945, two engines failing and the aircraft plunging into the sea just short of the beach

nese strip, which received the first B-29 on 12th October 1944. Aboard this plane was General Hansell, first chief of staff of the Twentieth Air Force and new commander of 21st Bomber Command. His primary combat unit at this time was the 73rd Bombardment Wing, commanded by General O'Donnell, who landed on Saipan on 18th October in the second B-29 to reach the island. Other Superfortresses followed at the rate of two to three a day during the next five weeks and, by 22nd November, more than one hundred were on hand.

The Command's first mission, a shakedown strike against the bypassed Japanese base at Truk, was flown on 27th October. Eighteen B-29s were launched, with Hansell piloting one of them. His bomber and three others, however, developed mechanical problems and were forced to return to Isley Field. The remaining fourteen B-29s proceeded to Truk, where they bombed from high altitude, each plane unloading about three tons of explosives on the island's submarine pens. The results were termed 'poor to fair'. During the strike, Japanese fighters made two passes at the bombers and there was some enemy antiaircraft fire, but no hits were scored. On 30th October and 2nd November two more shakedown missions were flown to Truk, with poor results.

The day the third mission was run, the Japanese launched their first preemptive strike against Isley Field. Twin-engine Betty bombers, staging out of Iwo Jima 600 miles to the north, came in low over the ocean and caught the Americans by surprise. The Japanese dropped several sticks of bombs which caused some minor damage to several parked B-29s. At least one enemy plane was shot down by antiaircraft fire. In response, Hansell ordered a mission against the Iwo Jima airfields on 5th November. Twenty-four Superfor-

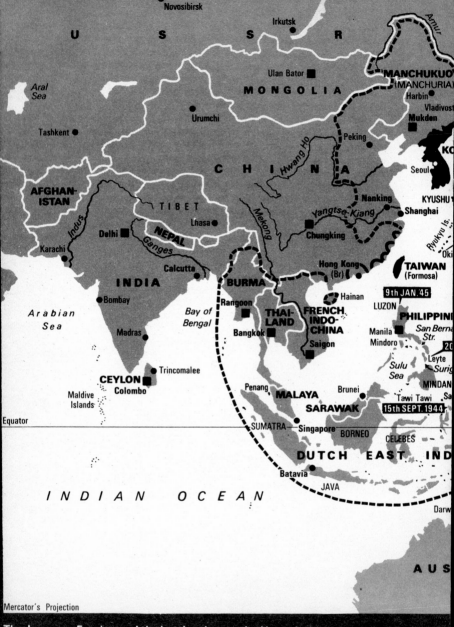

The Japanese Empire, and the battles that marked its reduction

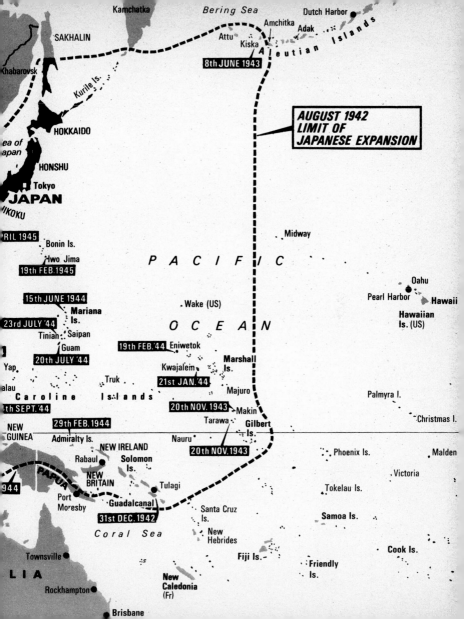

Like most other AAF Commands, the 21st Bomber Command adopted the habit of embellishing its aircraft with 'nose art', examples of this form of decoration applied to this Command's B-29s are seen on these pages

tresses, each carrying about five tons of bombs, hit the Japanese island from above 25,000 feet altitude. Ten missed the airfields entirely, due to a malfunction of the lead plane's bomb bay doors. The Japanese response was limited to light antiaircraft fire.

A second B-29 mission was flown against the Iwo Jima fields on 8th November with equally poor effect. The lead plane of eight bombers overran the identification point and all bombs missed the target. On this raid, eleven other B-29s were reported 'noneffective' because of various kinds of technical problems. The mission cost 21st Bomber Command its first loss, when one of the B-29s developed engine trouble and the pilot ditched into the ocean. Only two crewmen survived. The 8th November raid also flushed out some enemy fighter aircraft, which tried unsuccessfully to down the bombers using the air-to-air bombing tactic employed by Japanese pilots in Manchuria. The final shakedown mission of the Marianas aircrews was flown against Truk on 11th November. Eight planes unloaded in clear weather from 25,000 feet, with somewhat better results.

The next mission was scheduled for Tokyo. For this important operation, Twentieth Air Force changed target priorities. Up to this time, AAF planners had emphasized the destruction of Japan's steel industry, and steel plants had been repeatedly attacked by the B-29s based in China. They now listed Japan's aircraft industry as the top target of the B-29s. On 11th November, Major-General Lauris Norstad, Hansell's successor as chief of staff of the Twentieth Air Force, directed the first Tokyo strike be launched against the Nakajima Aircraft Company's Musashi plant. This company in 1944 manufactured thirty percent of all aircraft engines produced in Japan, second only to Mitsubishi Heavy Industries, Ltd. Reconnaissance photographs of the Musashi facility and many others had been brought back to Saipan on 1st November by a B-29 reconnaissance plane (known as the F-13), piloted by Captain Ralph D Steakley. Steakley's crewmen were the first Americans to fly over the Japanese capital since the Doolittle raid. They had orbited at 32,000 feet well above the range of Japanese fighters and antiaircraft fire, while their cameras ground away to give US air planners their first good look at Japanese industrial and military facilities in the Tokyo area. The appearance of the high-flying B-29 over the enemy capital clearly upset the normally seductive voice of Tokyo Rose, the Japanese-American propagandist. Broadcasting a warning to the men of the 21st, she declared: 'Sixty hours after the first bombs drop on Tokyo, there won't be an American alive on Saipan.'

Hansell scheduled the attack for 17th November. His plan called for the B-29s to bomb from 30,000 feet, with each plane unloading about twenty-five tons of ordnance, thirty percent incendiaries. Elaborate precautions were taken to deploy air-sea rescue units along the flight path between Saipan and Japan. Five submarines were stationed between the main island of Honshu and Iwo Jima and two destroyers south of the latter. In addition, several seaplanes were ordered to be either airborne or on base alert about the time the bombers were due back. To send word of the important mission to the world's press, twenty-four war correspondents were flown to Saipan. Early in the morning of 17th November, the crews boarded their aircraft and prepared for take-off. The weather, however, was poor and Hansell held up the departure hoping it would clear. Instead, it got worse and he was finally forced to cancel the operation. During the next five anxiety-ridden days – while Arnold fretted in Washington over the delay – the weather continued to frustrate the airmen. Finally, on the seventh day – 24th November – the wind shifted and,

**General Haywood S Hansell,
Commanding General of the 21st
Bomber Command**

as the skies began to clear, the first B-29 with General O'Donnell at the controls sped down the runway and lifted off. He was followed by 110 bombers, but seventeen of these were later forced to return because of mechanical problems.

If the week's delay had dulled the sensibilities of the crews, they soon grew tense and alert as the ninety-four bombers proceeded on toward Japan. Most of the airmen wore their winter flying equipment and flak suits, with oxygen masks hanging from the side of their helmets. Almost as soon as they reached the Japanese coast, Mount Fuji loomed up, its cone standing clear of scattered cumulus clouds. Nearing Tokyo at altitudes of 27,000 to 32,000 feet, the formations were swept into a 120 knot wind which gave the bombers a ground speed of about 445 miles per hour. On reaching the capital shortly after one o'clock in the afternoon, they found the Naka-jima plant almost completely obscured by an undercast and only twenty-four planes unloaded their bombs over the target, with the crews sighting sixteen bursts. Sixty-four other B-29s bombed the general urban area, while six aborted.

The crews on this first Tok[y] mission were relieved to find enem[y] fighter defenses less formidable th[an] they had feared. One observer lat[er] reported that the Japanese attemp[ts] at interception were 'laughable'. The[ir] fighters, he said, 'couldn't overtake [us] at our altitude and the flak trailed u[s]. Still, an enemy fighter managed [to bring] down one Superfortress, apparent[ly] by ramming. It crashed twenty mil[es] off the coast of Honshu with the lo[ss] of the entire crew. A second plane ra[n] out of gas on the return trip and ma[de] a three-point ocean landing into [a] twenty-foot swell. The crew quick[ly] scrambled out into life rafts and, f[or] the next ten hours, watched the B-[29] floating beside them, refusing to sin[k]. The crew was finally located by a B-[29] search plane and was picked up by a[n] American destroyer about twent[y] hours later. Eight other Superfor[t]-resses were damaged by enemy actio[n] and three were hit by other B-29 gun[s]. Based on information obtained fro[m] the crews, 21st Bomber Comma[nd] estimated more than one hundr[ed] Japanese fighters – a mixture of Tojo[s,] Zekes, Tonys, Nicks, Irvings, an[d] others – had attacked the B-29s an[d] that seven of them had been destroye[d] with eighteen probably destroyed, an[d] nine damaged.

But, as it turned out, the first Tok[yo] raid caused little damage to the ta[r]-get, although a bomb plot prepared b[y] the plant's management showed th[at] forty-eight, rather than sixtee[n] bombs fell in the factory area. Casua[l]-ties on the ground included fifty-seve[n] people killed and seventy-five injure[d.] Although the Japanese had bee[n] expecting the strike and had ordered [a] step-up in Tokyo air raid drills, suc[h] was the shock of the experienc[e,] according to a Foreign Office officia[l,] Toshikazu Kase, 'that the governmen[t] ceased to function' until the la[st] bombs had fallen. In Washingto[n,] General Arnold finally was able t[o] announce to the world that the Ameri-can air force had returned to Tokyo[.] The operation, he declared, was 'i[n] 'no sense a hit-and-run raid' such as Doolittle's. No matter where the Japanese might try to hide their factories, he promised that the Air Force would seek them out and destroy them. 'Japan has sowed the wind,' he said, 'now let it reap the whirlwind.'

On Saipan, after studying the post-strike reconnaissance photos, Hansell ordered the bombers out on a second daylight attack on the same target. On 27th November eighty-one B-29s were launched, nineteen almost at once 'non-effective'. The sixty-two other planes proceeded to Tokyo at high altitude but the crews were once more disappointed to find the target completely hidden by clouds. Forty-nine chose to bomb Tokyo's urban and dock areas by radar, while another seven struck at the Hammamatsu engine plant, halfway between the capital and Nagoya. On this mission, one B-29 ditched at sea with the loss of the entire crew. As the raid was under way, the Japanese struck again at Isley Field. Nine to eleven enemy aircraft, roaring in low from Iwo Jima, destroyed four parked B-29s, seriously damaged six, and put holes in twenty-two others. All but one of the enemy planes, however, were shot down by US antiaircraft fire and fighters. Following the Japanese counter-blow, Hansell ordered some of his bombers away from the crowded field at Isley to Guam, where three new airstrips – at North Field, North-west Field, and Depot Field – were under construction. He also consulted with Navy officials on Guam and a plan was devised for a combined strike on the enemy airstrips on Iwo Jima.

On 29th November, to keep up the pressure on the Japanese, twenty-nine bombers were sent on a night radar mission against Tokyo's dock and industrial areas. Twenty-three unloaded on the primary targets, two hit alternates, and four were non-effective. One B-29 was lost on the mission. On 3rd December another attempt was made to knock out the Nakajima facility in Tokyo. Seventy-six bombers reached Japan in clear weather but they caused little damage. During the raid Japanese fighters launched an estimated seventy-five attacks on the bombers and six were lost, at least four of which ditched at sea. One, rammed by a Tony, was badly damaged but made it back to base. B-29 gunners claimed ten of the enemy planes destroyed. Five days later Iwo Jima was hit in the first of two raids coordinated with a Navy bombardment of the island. The second B-29 strike was made on 24th December. The results of both raids were poor.

Not until the Command's twelfth mission on 13th December did Hansell see some substantial results from the B-29 effort. The target was the Mitsubishi engine plant at Nagoya, which was hit by 500-pound high explosives and some incendiaries dropped by seventy-one Superfortresses. Reconnaissance photos revealed that sixteen percent of the bombs fell within 1,000 feet of the aiming point and that more than seventeen percent of the facility's roofed area was destroyed. Actually, the damage was even worse, as totaled up by the Japanese. An assembly shop and seven auxiliary buildings at the number four engine works were destroyed and a second assembly shop and eleven other buildings were damaged. Also, a prototype engine manufacturing shop and two other buildings at the number two engine works were damaged. Japanese personnel losses came to 246 killed and many others injured. Plant officials estimated the attack reduced productive capacity from 1,600 engines per month to 1,200. Following the raid, the number four works no longer machined parts and its engine production was limited to assembling those parts already on hand or received from outside plants.

The raid also forced many Japanese aircraft companies to accelerate the dispersal of their manufacturing activities, which they had tentatively begun after the first raids from Saipan.

B-29s soften up a Japanese-held Pacific island in preparation for an Allied seaborne assault

As the bombings increased, the Japanese government later issued formal directives to the Nakajima and Mitsubishi management to further disperse their facilities to villages, woods, and underground sites outside the cities. As it turned out, this activity created more disruption to enemy aircraft production that the actual B-29 strikes themselves. This information, had it been available to the Americans on Saipan, would have eased the pain of the loss of four more B-29s during the 13th December raid. Two of them ditched at sea, one was presumed shot down by enemy flak, and one was lost to unknown causes.

On 18th December – the same day LeMay flew his successful incendiary strike against Hankow – Hansell sent his bombers back to Nagoya. The target was a giant Mitsubishi aircraft assembly plant, containing more than 4,250,000 square feet of floor space. Sixty-three B-29s bombed the primary target, most of them by radar because of a heavy cloud cover, with good results. More than seventeen percent of the roofed area was apparently destroyed and various other buildings extensively damaged. Japanese personnel losses, including dead and injured, came to more than 400. Despite the damage, the plant lost only ten days production. Four more B-29s were lost on the mission, two to unknown causes. Superfortress gunners claimed five enemy planes.

The day after the Hankow and Nagoya raids, Twentieth Air Force directed Hansell to launch a full-scale incendiary attack on Nagoya with one hundred B-29s. Norstad advised that the mission was an 'urgent requirement' for planning purposes. The B-29 commander protested the directive. In a personal message to Arnold, he pointed out that he had 'with great difficulty implanted the principle that our mission is the destruction of primary targets by sustained and determined attacks using precision bombing methods both visual and radar.' Just as this doctrine was beginning to get results, he said, he was asked to resort to area bombing which was not in his original mission directive. Replying for Arnold, Norstad said that the aircraft industry still had 'overriding priority' and that the test fire raid was 'simply a special requirement resulting from the necessity of future planning.' Hansell agreed to run the mission after completing operations previously scheduled. He was not alone in objecting to area bombing. Lieutenant-General Millard F Harman, commander of Army Forces in the Pacific Ocean Area – who later would lose his life in a plane crash near Kwajelein – argued that: 'Burning flimsy houses will not beat the Japs. Our targets are war industries. We want to stop them from making airplanes . . . to paralyze their power system and knock out their steel mills.' Harman also believed Tokyo could not be destroyed by incendiaries since, he noted, the Japanese were working feverishly to build huge firebreaks in the capital, some a block wide.

On 22nd December 21st Bomber Command returned to Nagoya in another raid on the Mitsubishi engine works. The planes carried only incendiaries, although the strike was not considered a response to Norstad's request. When the seventy-eight bombers reached the target area, once again they found it obscured by clouds and only forty-eight unloaded by radar on the plant, causing little damage. Three bombers were lost to vigorous enemy opposition, which included more than 500 fighter attacks. B-29 gunners claimed nine enemy aircraft destroyed. The final mission of the year, against the Nakajima plant in Tokyo, was a failure. Seventy-two planes took off for the capital on 27th December, but only thirty-nine reached and bombed the target, causing little damage. Three more B-29s were lost during the raid.

That day, 27th December, General Hansell issued a statement to the press in which he sought to sum up the Command's first month of operations. The results, he said, were encouraging but 'far from the standards we are seeking.' When his airmen failed 'to put bombs right on the primary target, they do not consider that they have done a good job.' He continued: 'The primary target is always a rather small section of enemy territory and it looks particularly small when seen from an altitude of something over five miles. Frequently you cannot see it because of clouds or overcast and must depend upon your instruments. We have not put all our bombs exactly where we wanted to put them and therefore we are not by any means satisfied with what we have done so far. We are still in our early, experimental stages. We have much to learn and many operational and other technical problems to solve. Some of our experiments, however, have been gratifying if not satisfying, and the B-29 has proved itself a magnificent weapon of war.'

This statement apparently struck General Arnold the wrong way, particularly Hansell's remark about considering himself still in an early, experimental stage with the new bomber. Only ten days earlier the press in America carried a war correspondent's story out of 20th Bomber Command headquarters in India which began: 'The experimental phase of B-29 operations is over. The Superfortress has proved itself as an airplane and as a weapon of war . . . As a result of six months of pioneering by the 20th Bomber Command, Superfortresses here and in the Pacific now can get down to a steady, efficient smashing of Japan's war potential.' Arnold apparently agreed with this view and, sometime around the first of the new year, he decided to replace Hansell with LeMay, in somewhat the same abrupt manner in which he had replaced Wolfe with LeMay.

To break the bad news, he dispatched General Norstad to the Marianas to see Hansell and he also ordered LeMay to fly there from India for the conference. Norstad arrived at 21st Bomber Command headquarters on Guam on 6th January and LeMay came in the following day. The three young generals – at forty-one Hansell was the oldest – knew each other well. LeMay had served under Hansell as a group commander in Great Britain and Norstad was his personal friend and had succeeded him as chief-of-staff of the Twentieth Air Force. The matter of the transfer of command was apparently quickly settled and LeMay departed for Kharagpur, taking with him Brigadier-General Roger M Ramey, Hansell's chief-of-staff, who would take charge of 20th Bomber Command. LeMay returned to Guam several weeks later, assuming his new command on 20th January.

Before returning to the States, where he would command a B-29 training wing, Hansell wrote a lengthy letter in which he summed up his command's operations during his brief tour. He suggested that, in comparison with the record of 20th Bomber Command, his record had not been too bad and he went on to list four major problems which he had faced: 1. converting the 73rd Wing from its preference for radar night bombing to precision bombing; 2. improving bombing accuracy, which he considered deplorable; 3. reducing the abort rate, running at twenty-one percent of sorties; and 4. reducing aircraft ditchings and improving air-sea rescue. This letter, as James Lea Cate and James C Olson have noted in the official AAF history, shed light on the reasons for his relief. That is, Hansell was still firmly committed to the doctrine of high-altitude, precision bombing.

But, unfortunately, it had not produced the promised results and there were growing pressures in Washington, not only from Arnold but from the President, to hurry the war's end. Roosevelt was particularly concerned about the expected huge casualties that would result from an invasion of the Japanese mainland, which the JCS was planning for late 1945. To reduce casualties, the President turned his attention more and more to the idea of an intensive aerial bombardment in order, as he told

Stalin on 8th February 1945, 'to be able to destroy Japan, and its army, and thus save lives.' The kind of intensive destruction Roosevelt envisioned in early 1945 could not be achieved by high-altitude precision bombing.

Prior to the change of command in the Marianas, Hansell on 3rd January 1945 launched the test incendiary mission against Nagoya which Norstad requested. Ninety-seven B-29s got airborne, each carrying about two and one-half tons of M-69 incendiary clusters, some of them fuzed to open at eight thousand feet, others at one thousand feet below releasing altitude. Fifty-seven bombers got over the city's docks and urban areas and bombed visually through a partial cloud cover. The bombs ignited some seventy-five fires and destroyed an estimated 140,000 square feet of the target. There was no holocaust, however, and the test seemed inconclusive. The mission cost the command five B-29s, one to enemy fighters and three to unknown causes. One plane ditched at sea.

Having carried out his special directive, Hansell during the last days in command returned to precision bombing of enemy aircraft and engine plants. On 9th January he sent seventy-two bombers against the Nakajima factory, but extremely high winds over Tokyo broke up the formations. Only eighteen B-29s hit the primary target, causing little damage, while thirty-four struck at alternate targets. Five more B-29s were lost on the raid: two were shot down by Japanese fighters, one ditched into the ocean on the way back to base, and two were lost to unknown causes. On 14th January the B-29s returned to the Mitsubishi plant at Nagoya and another five failed to return. Of the seventy-three that took off on the mission, only forty hit the primary target with 'fair' results.

A few days earlier, Arnold had complained to Hansell about the Superfortress losses:

'I am ... aware of the fact that some of these airplanes naturally must be ditched, but it seems on every raid there are three or four airplanes that go down. It would seem to me that as the losses from this cause are constant and, if added up, will present a large number, we should try to find the causes and determine what we can do to prevent them ... In my opinion, the B-29 cannot be treated in the same way we treat a fighter, a medium bomber, or even a flying fortress. We must consider the B-29 more in terms of a naval vessel, and we do not lose naval vessels in threes and fours without a very thorough analysis of the causes and what preventive measures may be taken to avoid losses in the future.'

Hansell disagreed with Arnold's analogy. In reply, he said that if the Navy committed its fleet of destroyers

B-29s of the 29th Bomb Group at dispersal on Northfield, Guam

five or six times a month, their losses would be prohibitive. In any event, he had already taken steps to cut losses through improved inspection and maintenance of the bombers. One of his most important actions in this connection was an aircraft weight reduction program, which stripped 1,900 pounds basic weight from the B-29, plus another 4,100 pounds by removing one of the bomb-bay tanks. The total weight reduction of 6,000 pounds had an immediate beneficial effect on aircraft performance, reducing power requirements and cutting down the burden on the engines.

The weight reduction effort may have helped on the final mission flown by 21st Bomber Command under Hansell. On 19th January a mission was flown in good weather against the Kawasaki Aircraft Plant at Akashi, twelve miles from Kobe, without a loss and produced what Cate and Olson declare was Hansell's 'first completely successful B-29 attack.' Sixty-two

bombers – making their runs at 25,000 to 27,000 feet – dropped 155 tons of ordnance on the Kawasaki factory. Reconnaissance photos confirmed a good strike, but the extent of the damage was not known until after the war. The bombers had hit every important building in both the engine and airframe branches and cut the plant's production by ninety percent. The mission proved that, when weather conditions were right (though they were rarely so over Japan), high altitude precision bombing could produce significant results.

After taking command on 20th January, LeMay made no immediate change in tactics and the five missions flown during the remainder of January all were high altitude precision strikes. One of these, on 27th January, cost 21st Bomber Command nine planes – the largest loss of any mission flown to that time. The target was the Nakajima plant, which had escaped serious damage despite repeated attacks. Seventy-four B-29s got airborne and headed for Tokyo, which once again was hidden by clouds. Fifty-six bombed by radar over the general urban area. The Japanese Air Force, apparently primed for the strike, attacked the Americans with 'unparalleled intensity.' During more than 900 passes, including many ramming attempts, enemy fighters shot down five B-29s and caused two others to ditch at sea. One bomber crashed on return to base and a ninth plane was lost to unknown causes.

Although the B-29 gunners claimed sixty enemy planes downed, it was after such costly missions as this that the morale of the crews took a nose dive. The situation led LeMay to propose to Washington switching his attacks from the heavily defended Nagoya and Tokyo areas to other targets. He specifically recommended an attack on Mitsubishi's aircraft works at Tamashima. In reply, Norstad suggested Kobe as an alternate target and he further directed that the bombers carry mostly incen-

diaries. Hansell's incendiary raid on Nagoya, he indicated, had not provided Washington planners sufficient information. LeMay scheduled his first February mission against Kobe, Japan's sixth largest city, containing the largest concentration of shipbuilding and marine engineering facilities in the country. For this operation, LeMay was able to draw upon the additional resources of a newly arrived B-29 Wing, the 313th, commanded by Brigadier-General John H Davies.

On 4th February one hundred B-29s were launched on the Kobe mission. The city was partly covered by clouds when sixty-nine bombers began their runs at 24,000 to 27,000 feet and dropped visually nearly 140 tons of incendiaries and thirteen tons of fragmentation bombs. Thirty of the B-29s hit alternate targets. Enemy air opposition over Kobe was aggressive. One bomber was shot down, thirty-five others were damaged, and another burned on landing at Saipan. Reconnaissance photos revealed damage exceeding the incendiary raid on Nagoya, with more than 2,500,000 square feet of Kobe's built-up area destroyed or damaged. According to postwar information, more than 1,000 buildings were burned out or seriously damaged in the industrial southwestern district of Kobe. Local war production was hard hit and one of the two major shipyards was forced to cut its operations in half.

While the results of the Kobe attack were being evaluated, plans were moving forward to seize Iwo Jima from the Japanese. Enemy aircraft based on the island had continued their attacks on Saipan. In all, through December 1944, more than eighty Japanese planes raided Isley Field and managed to destroy a total of eleven B-29s, caused major damage to eight, and minor damage to thirty-five. About thirty-seven of the raiders were shot down. The Japanese took much satisfaction from these raids. The newspaper *Mainichi* claimed that ten percent of the B-29s in Saipan had been put out of action by the Japanese strikes. When it added that number to those B-29s claimed shot down or damaged over Japan and Manchuria, plus American operational losses, the Japanese newspaper estimated the United States had lost 760 Superfortresses and more than 5,000 airmen. (Actual B-29 losses by 1st January 1945, to all causes, were 150 planes and 891 men.)

Iwo Jima, however, remained troublesome for reasons other than the air attacks on Saipan. Because of the threat of the Japanese fighters based there, the B-29s were forced to fly a dog-leg to avoid them, which required more fuel and reduced their bomb loads. Furthermore, the island's radar gave early warning of B-29s en route to the homeland. After considering these factors, the JCS decided to seize Iwo Jima. In American hands it would not only end the interference with B-29 operations, but could also be used as a base for long-range fighters which could accompany the B-29s on strike missions to Japan and as an intermediate landing strip for crippled bombers. On 27th January LeMay conferred with Admiral Nimitz and General Harman on plans for softening up Iwo Jima's defenses before D-Day, 19th February. On the 12th, twenty-one B-29s joined Navy units in attacks on the island, dropping eighty-four tons of bombs. As part of the Iwo operation, the fast carriers of Task Force 58, under Vice Admiral Marc A Mitscher, steamed toward Japan to launch the Navy's first air strikes against Tokyo, while simultaneously surface forces under Rear Admiral W H P Blandy converged on the island.

As part of 21st Bomber Command's indirect support of the invasion, Le-May on 15th February sent the B-29s against the Mitsubishi Engine Works at Nagoya. Thirty-three bombers hit the primary target, while fifty-four attacked the Nakajima engine plant at Hammamatsu. One B-29 was lost on the mission after ditching into the ocean. In the meantime, Blandy's Task Force moved into position off Iwo Jima and his battleships and cruisers opened up a bombardment on 16th February – the same day that about 1,000 sorties from Mitscher's carriers were flown against Tokyo. After launching follow-up attacks on the 17th, Mitscher immediately turned his carriers around and headed back to Iwo Jima to join in support of the 19th February landings. A Marine division hit the beaches northeast of Suribachi in the morning and, by day's end, some 30,000 troops were ashore. The epic story of Iwo Jima – which featured a fierce resistance by the Japanese troops – has become part of the Marine heritage. The final victory was costly to them and the United States: they suffered 20,196 casualties, including 4,189 killed. The Japanese, who fought almost to the last man, lost 21,000 dead. The island was declared secured on 15th March 1945. Iwo Jima's loss was another severe blow to the Japanese since it was an actual part of Tokyo prefecture.

Long before the battle ended, Navy Seebee units landed to begin the job of rebuilding the battered Japanese airfields. One strip became available for observation planes on 26th February, another was graded to four thousand feet by early March, just in time to serve as an emergency field for a B-29 in distress, which landed on the 4th after a mission to Tokyo. P-51 fighters moved up to Iwo Jima on 6th March and, in early April, escorted the Superfortresses for the first time to the mainland. From the viewpoint of the B-29 crews, however, the primary value of Iwo Jima was that it provided them a place to land between Honshu and the Marianas. In all, before the war ended, 2,251 B-29s would land there. With completion of the Iwo operation, and with the number of Superfortresses increasing steadily in the Marianas, the stage was set for the accelerated bombing assault on Japan.

Tokyo...as bright as sunrise

After American forces stormed ashore on the island of Luzon on 9th January 1945, the Japanese high command promulgated a new directive – approved by the Emperor on the 20th – to guide future homeland defense operations. It called for continued resistance by the Japanese army in the Philippines to delay the Americans' approach to the country's main defense perimeter. This perimeter was identified as a line running along the 25th parallel from Iwo Jima due west to Formosa. Above that line steps were to be taken to strengthen strong points at Shanghai, on the south Korean coast, and in the Ryukyuan chain, with the work to be completed during February and March. The Japanese planned that the main defense effort would center on Okinawa in the Ryukyus.

This work, however, had scarcely gotten under way when the eastern end of the perimeter was unhinged by American amphibious forces invading Iwo Jima on 19th February. That same day also was important in the history of B-29 operations from the Marianas. On the 19th Twentieth Air Force headquarters issued a new directive to LeMay which soon drastically changed the course of the aerial bombardment campaign; it elevated 'test' incendiary raids to a priority above attacks on the Japanese aircraft industry. To carry them out, the B-29 commander had available an additional wing of Superfortresses under Brigadier-General Thomas S Power. Several days later LeMay ordered the first incendiary raid against Tokyo. On 25th February 172 B-29s – the largest force to strike Japan up to that time – dropped 450 tons of incendiaries from high altitudes through a heavy cloud cover. The damage was substantial: post-strike photos indicated one square mile of the city had been demolished. According to Tokyo metropolitan police records, the raid leveled a total of 27,970 buildings. The Command lost six planes on the mission, two to enemy aircraft ramming.

In Tokyo the day following this strike, Emperor Hirohito received in audience former Premier Tojo to obtain his views on the general war situation. For several weeks the Emperor had called in other Japanese elder statesmen for the same purpose. With only one exception – Prince Konoye, who believed the war was lost – all of them indicated that Japan should continue to fight on. On the 26th Tojo informed the Emperor he was not worried about the B-29 raids or Japan's prospects. He estimated that the Americans could not increase their bomber raids or even continue the current rate of attacks, which he saw as 'insignificant' compared to the raids the Allies were launching against Germany. Only if Tokyo were being bombed day after day, by several thousand planes based closer to Japan, he said, would the situation be comparable. Instead, Japan was faced with an attack about once a week by one hundred or so B-29s, coming from bases 'well in excess of 2,000 kilometres'. If the Japanese people were discouraged by such a 'small matter,' then achieving Japan's goals in the Greater East Asia War would be impossible. The former minister of war and chief of the army general staff clearly reflected the attitude of Imperial General Headquarters, which was girding for the 'decisive' battle of the homeland.

Neither Tojo, nor his army colleagues, could foresee the great calamity that was about to overtake Japan. Beforehand, there was a brief interregnum. On 4th March, a week after the high altitude incendiary raid, 21st Bomber Command flew

B-29s were greeted over Japan by heavy fighter opposition, and here a twin-engined Kawasaki Ki-45 Toryu of the Japanese Army Air Force (known as 'Nick' to the B-29 crews) slips beneath the wing of a Superfortress (top centre) after completing its firing pass, just missing the giant plane's propellers

Principal B-29 fire raids and the two atomic strikes on Japan

NIIGATA

FIRST FIRE RAID:
25th FEBRUARY 1945
GREAT FIRE RAID
NIGHT 9/10th MARCH
124,000 CASUALTIES

H O N S H U

HITACHI

NANAO

UTSUNOMIYA ●

MITO

FUSHIKI ● TOYAMA

MAEBASHI ● ● ISESAKI
KUMAGAYA ●

FIRE RAIDS:
NIGHT 11th/12th MARCH
& 19th MARCH

HACHIOJI ● **TOKYO** ● CHOSHI

● FUKUI

KOFU ● **KAWASAKI**
YOKOHAMA

CHIBA

ZU

TSURUGA

HIRATSUKA ●

GIFU
OGAKI ● ICHINOMIYA

NUMAZU ●

MAISURU

KUWANA

NAGOYA

SHIMIZU ●

SHIZUOKA

OKAZAKI ●

AMAGASAKI

YOKKAICHI

TOYOHASHI ●

● **HAMAMATSU**

KOBE

FIRE RAID:
NIGHT 14th/15th MARCH
13,000 CASUALTIES

ASHI

OSAKA

● **WAKAYAMA**

USSR

Japanese terr-
itories Mar. 1945

MANCHURIA

KOREA

JAPAN
Tokyo

Peking ●

P A C I F I C

CHINA

O C E A N

Shanghai ●

● Nagasaki

Yakoshima

**FIGHTER
BASE**

Ryukyu Is.

Okinawa

Iwo Jima ●

I C

N

● Hong Kong

FORMOSA

1,600 miles

MARIANA IS.

**PHILIPPINE
IS.**

Saipan
Tinian
Guam

**B 29 BOMBER
BASES**

**B 29 BASE
FOR ATOM BOMB
ATTACKS**

another mission that continued the old pattern and must have confirmed Tojo in his opinions. This mission was a high altitude daylight precision strike aimed once more at destroying the Nakajima aircraft plant in Tokyo. 159 B-29s reached the target area only to find it hidden again from view by clouds and they bombed by radar, unloading 500 tons of high explosives. When the dust settled, the Nakajima plant still stood virtually intact. After eight missions by 875 bombers, it had suffered only four percent damage and much of this was attributed to a single strike by Navy carrier planes made a few weeks before. The failure of the 4th March raid seemed conclusive evidence that high altitude, precision bombing was generally futile. Not one of the AAF's high priority enemy aircraft or engine plants had been put entirely out of action, although one had been badly crippled and another forced to severely curtail production. The postwar United States Strategic Bombing Survey (USSBS) attributed the failure of the early B-29 campaign partly to the AAF's continued adherence to the doctrine of precision bombing.

However, as we have noted elsewhere, the early raids did produce significant indirect results. They forced the enemy to disperse his aircraft industry and this cut heavily into airframe and engine production and development. At the beginning of 1945, for example, both the Japanese army and navy were working desperately to develop attack aircraft for use both against the B-29s and the Allied homeland invasion fleet. One such aircraft under development was a Navy turbo jet which resembled the German Messerschmitt Me-262 fighter. Inspection of the mockup was conducted on 25th January 1945. However, in response to the B-29 attacks, the Tokyo plant where the plane was being worked on was dispersed to various farm hutments outside the capital and it was not until April that the Japanese were able to resume

development. The first model was completed on 25th June and the first test flight, with a new engine, was made on 7th August, shortly before Japan's surrender. While it is unlikely that this and other new Japanese aircraft would have changed the outcome, the fact remains that they dismantled and dispersed about one hundred aircraft plants. This activity, USSBS found, resulted in production losses 'greater than that due to direct air attacks.'

The extent of this disruption was unknown to Arnold and Norstad who, prior to March 1945, had begun to worry that the B-29 was not living up to its original billing. We have mentioned some of the reasons for the generally poor bombing. Bad weather was a constant factor, including the extremely high winds, some in the order of 180 miles an hour, which made precision bombing difficult. Frequent cloud cover exasperated the crews, who rarely had a clear view of the targets. The high bombing altitudes also reduced B-29 effectiveness since only relatively small tonnages could be carried due to the need for heavy gasoline loads to operate at 25,000 feet and above. Japanese opposition had proved only an indirect cause of the poor bombing results. Of seventy-eight B-29s lost on combat missions between November 1944 and March 1945, fifty-three were caused by mechanical (mostly engine) failure rather than enemy action.

As he reviewed his situation in early March, and discussed with his wing commanders and staff the problem of hitting Japan harder, LeMay conceived a major and dramatic change in tactics. He decided to remove all guns and ammunition from the bombers on the next mission, and to leave behind all gunners (except the tail gunners, who would serve as observers) to lighten the Superfortresses and enable them to carry more incendiaries. Further, he proposed to attack at night at altitudes of 5-6,000 feet. The planes were to go in individually, rather than in formation, and be guided to the target area by pathfinder planes sent ahead to start initial fires.

General Power, commander of the 314th Wing, Colonel John B Montgomery, his assistant chief of staff, and others endorsed LeMay's plan but, not unexpectedly, as a squadron historian later wrote, it 'met with considerable misgivings by the combat crews.' The airmen, grown accustomed to what they believed was the safety of high altitude bombing, were fearful that they would become sitting ducks for Japanese antiaircraft guns. However, LeMay had studied the statistics on losses to enemy flak and they were not impressive. He argued that Japanese antiaircraft defenses would not be effective at medium and low altitudes and also that the enemy did not have much of a night fighter capability. Still, he was not unaware of the danger. Realizing that he was taking a calculated risk, he decided to assume full responsibility for the operation by delaying submission of his plan to Washington. If there was a disaster, then Arnold would be blameless and free to fire him.

LeMay scheduled the strike against Tokyo for the evening of 9th March – almost exactly one year after the Battle of Kansas, which had been fought to get the B-29s combat-ready and deployed overseas. The day before the mission was flown, General Norstad arrived at 21st Bomber Command headquarters to discuss future operations. After he was briefed on the new strike plan, Norstad wired Washington to prepare 'for an outstanding show'. For the mission, LeMay had on hand in the Marianas 385 B-29s. The lead planes, including one flown by General Power, took off in the late afternoon, loaded with M-47 incendiaries. Those that followed carried the M-69 clusters, in all, 2,000 tons of incendiaries.

Darkness had settled over both the Marianas and Japan hours before the first of the 279 Superfortresses arrived over the target. On Guam, LeMay and several members of his staff waited up for the report of bombs away. The pathfinder planes reached the capital shortly after midnight. Going in at the planned low altitudes, they began dropping their incendiaries on a highly congested rectangular area approximately ten miles square, bordering the most important industrial section of Tokyo. Fires were ignited immediately and formed an almost perfect X. The weather, so often a handicap to the B-29s, now made a contribution. Just prior to bombs away, a high wind arose which fanned the flames and spread them rapidly. As other B-29s reached the city and also unloaded, additional fires were started. The winds increased to twenty-eight miles per hour, sending burning debris leaping over fire breaks and canals.

The individual fires soon merged into one vast mass of flames that burned so furiously that bombers approaching the target saw the glow forty miles away. Some of the late arrivals flew through huge clouds of smoke which blackened their fuselages and gun blisters with soot. When bomb bay doors were opened, the smell of burning buildings invaded the aircraft. The holocaust also generated violent air currents, which hurled several B-29s skyward thousands of feet in seconds. Crewmen were flung from their seats and some struck their heads violently against the fuselages, saved from serious injury only by their helmets.

The raid continued for about two hours while General Power's plane – having dropped its bomb load early and climbed high above the attacking Superfortresses – orbited the city while he and the crew carefully observed the operation and attempted to collect data for later evaluation. Via radio Power sent cryptic reports to LeMay on the conflagration, which made a tremendous and lasting impression on him. But on the ground, the scene was much worse, a nightmare out of Dante's inferno. Radio

Vast areas of the Kanda and Nihonbashi in Tokyo were gutted by the incendiary raids of B-29s as seen above, but the B-29s did not have things all their own way as may be seen left – a battle-damaged B-29 burning after making a crash landing on the Iwo Jima airstrip following a Tokyo raid

Tokyo broadcast an account some hours later in which the announcer, after condemning the Americans for 'a slaughter' of the people, vividly described the disaster:

'That bright starlight night will remain in the memory of all who witnessed it. After the first incendiary bombs fell, clouds formed and were lit up from below with a pink light. From them emerged Superfortresses, flying uncannily low above the centers of conflagration, which gradually spread. A B-29 exploded before our eyes like a magnesium tracer bullet, almost over the center of the city. The fire-clouds kept creeping higher

and the tower of the Diet building stood black against the red sky. The city was as bright as at sunrise; clouds of smoke, soot, even sparks driven by the storm, were flying over it. That night we thought the whole of Tokyo was reduced to ashes...'

The raid of 10th March proved to be one of the greatest disasters ever suffered by any belligerent in the history of warfare. In a single night, the B-29s destroyed almost sixteen square miles of the heart of Tokyo. Nearly twenty-five percent of all buildings in the capital – 267,171 structures – were demolished. Witnesses stated that the heat was so intense that entire block fronts burst into flames before the main body of fire reached them. Combustible contents of concrete buildings burned completely, leaving no evidence of what they were. Casualties were enormous, with more people being killed that night than would die in the atomic blasts at either Hiroshima or Nagasaki. According to figures compiled by the Japanese metropolitan police, 83,783 people were killed, 40,918 were injured, and more than 1,000,000 people were left homeless. It took the Japanese authorities twenty-five days to remove all the blackened corpses. B-29 losses on the strike totalled fourteen, at least one of which was shot down by Japanese flak batteries and was seen crashing with a great explosion. The crews of five bombers ditched into the ocean and were saved by air-sea rescue units.

Eighteen hours after the attack, Premier Koiso spoke over Radio Tokyo to denounce the 'most cruel and barbaric Americans' and to warn the Japanese people to expect still more B-29 bombings. He also reported to them that the United States was planning to invade the homeland. In the Marianas, LeMay – who received a wire of congratulations from Arnold – was already planning another low-level night attack, this time against Nagoya. On this mission on 11th-12th March, 285 bombers struck the city

Above: M-69 incendiary clusters are loaded aboard a B-29 on Saipan prior to a mission. *Below:* A complete load of 184 M-47 incendiary bombs such as could be lifted by a B-29 if no auxiliary fuel was carried. *Right:* The pilot of 'Easy's Aces' inspects his crew before taking-off from Guam for Japan

from low altitudes, the pathfinder planes again leading the way with M-47 incendiaries. In all, they dropped 1,700 tons on Nagoya and started hundreds of fires. On this occasion, there was no general holocaust but post-strike photos showed more than two square miles of the city leveled. One bomber was lost on the mission and twenty-four damaged, mostly by flak. Fighter opposition was weak.

Two nights later, after having worked his maintenance crews around the clock, LeMay sent 300 B-29s to Osaka, Japan's second city in population and industrial production. Bombing by radar because of a cloud cover, 274 B-29s unloaded 1,700 tons of incendiaries. Although the weather had prevented the pathfinder planes from setting off spotting fires, the post-strike photos of Osaka confirmed that the new low-level attacks were paying off. More than eight square miles of the heart of the city had been gutted. The fires burned out 134,744 residential and industrial buildings and partly destroyed another 1,300 structures. Casualties totalled 13,135 with more than 500,000 people made

⸱omeless, a quarter of the city's ⸱opulation. Two B-29s were lost and ⸱hirteen damaged on this raid. Again, ⸱nemy air opposition was slight.

LeMay's fourth incendiary target, ⸱obe, was hit on the night of 16th-17th ⸱arch. The pilots were directed to ⸱ake a more controlled run to ensure ⸱oncentration and merging of the ⸱res. Because the Bomber Command's ⸱nventory of M-69s and M-47s was ⸱nning low, the bomb load was ⸱anged somewhat. In their place, ⸱0-pound clusters of four-pound mag⸱sium thermite (M-15) incendiaries ⸱re used. The Kobe raid was the ⸱aviest launched by LeMay up to ⸱at time. 307 B-29s hit the city with ⸱300 tons of bombs, setting off fires ⸱at leveled about three square miles ⸱ one end of the business district, ⸱us some industrial and residential ⸱eas. More than 66,000 structures, ⸱cluding 500 industrial buildings, ⸱re demolished. 250,000 people – a ⸱ird of Kobe's population – were left ⸱meless. Deaths and injuries came to ⸱000.

The last of the March 1945 fire raids – against Nagoya on the 9th – was flown by 290 bombers. With the inventory of incendiaries almost exhausted, every third plane was loaded with 500-pound high explosive bombs. The planes hit the north-central part of the city with about 1,800 tons of bombs, which started 192 separate fires and destroyed three square miles of the city. In all, during the two raids on Nagoya, five square miles were leveled. LeMay was highly pleased and issued a statement to his airmen, praising them for 'inspired devotion to duty'. The test of battle, he said, 'has established that you can not only withstand every stress, but that you can repeatedly strike with increased power.'

A few days later, in Washington, General Norstad told a press conference that the cost of the five raids to the Japanese was 'the greatest ever inflicted upon any people' in such a short period. In all, thirty-two square miles of urban area in four key Japanese cities had been destroyed. The incendiary attacks, he said, were merely the 'initial phase' of the B-29 campaign to wipe out the small home industries supporting the Japanese war effort. He paid special tribute to LeMay 'for solving an acute operational problem by using high altitude Superfortresses at low level to achieve the unloading of a large tonnage of bombs in a short time.' The home industries were indeed destroyed with everything else. Twenty-nine percent of all aircraft production in Japan had been carried out by subcontractors, concentrated in the Tokyo, Osaka, Nagoya industrial areas. These ranged in size from shops employing ten people to those hiring 2,000. Japanese officials later declared that the destruction of the smaller industries in the fire raids caused 'serious losses in production.'

By the end of March 21st Bomber Command had completely run out of incendiaries and did not fly another fire raid for some three months.

Support missions and urban area incendiary raids

In late March 1945, while Washington took emergency steps to refill the depleted incendiary stocks in the Marianas, 21st Bomber Command was diverted to support the Navy before and after the invasion of Okinawa. Some five months earlier, when the preliminary plans for the Okinawa operation were being prepared, AAF officials agreed that the B-29s would be made available to fly reconnaissance over the island and to strike enemy airfields on Kyushu in an effort to prevent Japanese planes from attacking the US invasion fleet. The final plan for 21st Bomber Command

support was discussed by LeMay and Navy representatives at Nimitz's headquarters on Guam on 7th March. The specific targets on Kyushu, however, were selected by LeMay and approved by Arnold. The two airmen agreed that the B-29s would aim their attacks at the enemy's permanent installations on Kyushu, rather than the airfields themselves 'except when unusual concentrations of aircraft exist or in case of emergency.'

On 27th March the Command flew the first raid of this series. 151 bombers hit at airfield facilities on Kyushu at Tachiari and Oita and the Omura aircraft plant, causing substantial damage. On the 31st another 137 B-29s struck Tachiari again and also plastered a Japanese facility at Omura. During this strike enemy fighters were up but scored only fifteen hits. One B-29 ditched on the way to the target. The following morning, D-Day, American assault troops stormed the beaches on Okinawa's west coast to begin the final and most costly battle of the Pacific war. When it had finally ended in June, the United States had lost 12,520 men killed and 36,631 wounded. The Japanese toll was 109,000 killed and 7,800 taken prisoner.

During and after the US landing on the island, the Japanese sent hundreds of *Kamikaze* aircraft against the huge American fleet off shore. As he began to take losses, Admiral Nimitz requested LeMay to hit the Kyushu fields, from where he believed the suicide planes originated. The B-29 crews responded by repeatedly plastering enemy strips at Izumi, Tachiari, Kokubu, Kanoya, and Nittagahara. However, it proved impossible to prevent the *Kamikaze* planes from continuing their attacks. Between 2nd April and 22nd June the Japanese launched about 1,900 suicide planes, which succeeded in sinking twenty-five Allied ships and scored several

21st Bomber Command B-29s disgorge their lethal cargoes over the industrial heart of Yokohama

Code-named 'Tojo' by the US Forces, the Kakajima Ki-44 Shoki was the only type of interceptor available in strength to the JAAF when B-29s launched their offensive against the Japanese mainland. The photos above show the widely-used Ki-44-IIb model. *Left:* The Japanese Foreign Minister Shigenori Togo

hundred other damaging hits. In this emergency, about seventy-five percent of the B-29s combat effort was aimed at the Kyushu airfields. LeMay, after a while, thought the repeated missions had become unproductive since the bombers had turned every runway on Kyushu into rubble.

When he queried Washington about the matter, he was directed to pursue the same course. The attacks on the Kyushu airfields, Washington inform- ed him on 18th April and again on 5th May, 'continue to have the first priority of the operations' of his Command. But finally, on 11th May 1945, Admiral Nimitz agreed to release the bombers to return to their own operations. He sent LeMay a message of appreciation.

Despite the diversion of the Super- fortresses during this period, the Command had been able to take the first steps towards implementing a new target directive received from Washington in early April. This directive, while continuing to give high priority to the destruction of the Nakajima and Mitsubishi engine works, designated certain urban areas in Tokyo, Kawasaki, Nagoya, and Osaka for incendiary attacks. When those specific targets had been destroyed, the Command was to begin a second series of raids against other targets in Tokyo, Yokohama, Kawa- saki, Kobe, Amagasaki, Osaka, and Nagoya. Having received new stocks of incendiaries, LeMay began the new series of raids on 13th April with a strike on Tokyo's arsenal area, north- west of the Imperial Palace. 327 B-29s dropped 2,100 tons of incendiaries, which burned out an additional eleven square miles of the city. Seven B-29s were lost on the mission. Two nights later, 300 Superfortresses returned to the capital area to blast urban targets in Tokyo, nearby Kawasaki, and Yokohama. They left behind ten square miles of destruction along the west shore of Tokyo bay. Japanese fighter opposition was 'moderate to heavy' and thirteen bombers were lost. Returning crews reported numerous B-29s went down 'in flames over the target.' One plane crashed at Iwo Jima.

By mid-April the strength of LeMay's forces had grown substantially with the arrival of two new wings, the 58th from India, and the 315th from the United States. For the first time he would be capable of launching 500 or more planes. At the end of April, he advised Norstad that he proposed to use his more powerful force to further intensify the air campaign. For the first time in the war against Japan, he said, the AAF had an opportunity to prove 'the power of the strategic air arm.' With his increased B-29 strength, he believed 21st Bomber Command could destroy Japan's ability to wage war 'providing its maximum capacity is exerted unstintingly during the next six months.'

It was with this goal in mind that LeMay initiated a new series of fire raids several days after the Command was relieved of the Okinawa support mission. It began with a massive daylight attack on 14th May on the northwestern section of Nagoya, site of the Mitsubishi engine works and other war industries. More than 500 B-29s took off on the mission, but fifty aborted. 472 Superfortresses went on to hit the primary target with 2,500 tons of M-69 incendiaries, starting many fires which leveled more than three square miles of the city, includ- ing the site of a bearing plant at the Mitsubishi number ten engine works. The raid, however, cost the Command eleven bombers: two to aggressive but uncoordinated enemy fighter attacks, four to accidents, and five to unknown causes. Fifty-four B-29s suffered flak damage. Two days later, the B-29s returned to Nagoya to unload 3,600 tons of incendiaries on the city's dock and industrial areas. They destroyed another four square miles and heavily damaged Mitsubishi's number five aircraft works. The two strikes led to another mass exodus from Nagoya, as an additional 170,000 people fled its ruins for the safety of the countryside.

On 23rd and 25th May the Superfortresses returned to Tokyo. On the first raid, 520 bombers reached the capital in the early morning hours and unloaded 3,600 tons of incendiaries on an area south of the Imperial Palace, along the west side of Tokyo harbor. The bombardiers had been specifically instructed to stay away from the Imperial Palace. During the raid about sixty Japanese fighters took on the Superfortresses, which also were buffeted by a terrific barrage of flak. The result was the heaviest losses in 21st Bomber Command history to that time. Seventeen B-29s were lost on the raid and sixty-nine were damaged. LeMay ordered a follow-up strike two nights later by another 500 bombers – and suffered even worse losses when twenty-six Superfortresses failed to return from the mission. However, the bombers managed to drop another 3,200 tons of incendiaries on the capital. These two raids gutted an additional eighteen square miles of Tokyo.

During the second raid on 25th May – despite the precautions taken by the Americans – the Imperial Palace was set ablaze by flying debris which leaped the moat. The Emperor and Empress were in their air raid shelter beneath the palace grounds at the time and were never in danger. However, twenty-eight members of the palace staff lost their lives in the fires, which burned about fourteen hours. The two May attacks temporarily paralyzed the capital and, according to Japanese officials, were a severe blow to the morale of the people, who realized the Japanese Air Force was unable to stop the B-29 onslaught. The damage caused brought the total destruction in Tokyo to more than fifty percent of the entire city area. Fifty-six square miles of the capital had been demolished.

LeMay considered the additional damage done worth the heavy loss of B-29s. However, because of the great concern within his headquarters, he ordered a change of tactics for the

next strike against Yokohama on 29th May. On this occasion, the planes were to go in at high altitude around the noon hour and also – to counter Japanese fighters – he brought in an escort of Iwo Jima-based P-51 Mustangs. Because these fighters lacked navigational equipment for the long overwater flight, a procedure had been devised whereby several B-29s would rendezvous with the P-51s over Kita, a pinpoint volcanic island about forty miles north of Iwo Jima. From there the Superfortresses would lead the fighters across the 600 mile stretch of ocean to Japan. The navigational B-29s would later rendezvous with the P-51s at a designated 'Rally Point' and escort them home.

It was fortunate the Mustangs were along since, as the Superfortresses reached the Yokohama area, 150 enemy fighters sought to interdict them. In the ensuing dog fight, the Mustangs claimed twenty-six Japanese planes shot down, nine damaged, and twenty-three probably destroyed, at a cost of only three P-51s. While the air battle raged, 454 bombers unloaded 2,500 tons of incendiaries on the port city, destroying nearly seven square miles of the main business district along the waterfront. Four B-29s were

lost due to enemy action: three to flak and one to a Japanese fighter which intentionally rammed it.

On 1st June LeMay sent the bombers against urban targets in the cities of Osaka and Kobe. A fighter escort was again called in but ran into unexpected trouble. The P-51s from Iwo hit a severe weather front, tried to punch through to the rendezvous point, and in the process many planes collided and twenty-seven went down at sea. Only a few dozen Mustangs managed to get through and to eventually join 458 B-29s over Osaka. Another strong Japanese fighter force attempted to interdict them, making hundreds of passes. The Americans also were greeted by heavy antiaircraft fire. Five B-29s were lost to flak and five more to other causes. Nevertheless, the Superfortresses were still able to unload 2,700 tons of M-69s on the northwest area of the city, burning out an additional three square miles. Eighty-one B-29s landed on Iwo Jima on the return flight.

Four days later the Superfortresses hit Kobe. During this raid, approximately 125 enemy fighters attacked the bombers, but were able to down only three. Three others were lost to flak and one crashed at Iwo Jima. Despite the attacks, most of the 400

Part of the 11th Naval Air Arsenal's underground machine shop at Hiro

B-29s hit the city with 3,000 tons of incendiaries, burning out more than four square miles and destroying 51,399 buildings, including four major war factories. After studying the post-strike photos of the damage, 21st Bomber Command analysts eliminated Kobe from the list of incendiary targets. The third and fourth raid of the series were flown on 7th and 15th June, both against Osaka. On the 7th 400 B-29s dropped 2,500 tons of bombs on the city. On the 15th they struck with another 3,100 tons. According to Japanese officials, the three June raids on Osaka caused more industrial damage than the fire raids of the previous March.

When the B-29s had completed this phase of the urban bombing campaign, Japan's six most important industrial cities – Tokyo, Nagoya, Kobe, Osaka, Yokohama, and Kawasaki – lay in ruins. Of a total urban area of 257·2 square miles in the six cities, the Superfortresses had destroyed 105·6. Many great factories had been burned out or rendered inoperative. Millions of Japanese had lost their homes. The civilian leadership of the country finally began, somewhat tentatively,

141

to reassert itself and to discuss ways and means to end the war. A new cabinet under Admiral Kantaro Suzuki – who took over from Koiso as Premier in April – agreed to seek Moscow's intercession at the proper time. However, it was not until July that the Japanese Foreign Minister, Shigenori Togo, formally directed his ambassador in Moscow, Naotake Sato, to request the assistance of the Soviet government in bringing about an end to the war. But even at this late date, the Japanese saw themselves as playing a role in 'establishing and maintaining lasting peace.'

Thus, in his instructions to Sato, the Foreign Minister stated that 'as long as America and England insist on unconditional surrender, our country has no alternative but to see [the war] through in an all-out effort for the sake of survival and the honor of the homeland.' To Ambassador Sato, Tokyo's view of the world situation seemed quite unrealistic. There was not the slightest possibility, he informed his superiors, of getting the Soviet Union to go along with any Japanese proposals. Furthermore, he said, England and America were planning to 'take the right of maintaining peace away from Japan.' He asked: 'In these days, with the enemy air raids accelerated and intensified, is there any meaning in showing our country has reserve strength for a war of resistance, or in sacrificing the lives of hundreds of thousands of conscripts and millions of other innocent residents of cities and metropolitan areas?' But the fact was that Imperial General Headquarters was already girding for such a war of resistance.

In addition to the urban area raids on Japan's principal cities, 21st Bomber Command in the spring of 1945 also launched a number of selective high altitude precision bombing strikes. One of the most spectacular of these took place on 7th April, when 153 bombers dropped 600 tons of high explosives from 16,000 to 25,000 feet on the Mitsubishi aircraft engine works at Nagoya and virtually leveled it. Although post-strike photos showed only sixty-two percent of the roofed area destroyed, actually ninety percent of the plant's facilities were ruined in this raid. The same day, another one hundred bombers hit the Nakajima plant in Tokyo with 2,000 pound bombs, just arrived in the theater. They caused heavy damage to machine shops and destroyed ten percent of the plant's facilities. A follow-up daylight raid on the Nakajima works on 12th April by ninety-three bombers added substantially to the destruction. According to a Nakajima official, the two April raids had 'devastating effects on buildings, machine tools, and the morale of the people.'

Japan's oil refineries and fuel storage facilities also came under B-29 attack in the spring of 1945. During the initial strike on 10th May, 300 bombers hit the Tokuyama naval fuel station and coal yard, the Otake oil refinery, and Oshima's oil storage facilities. The damage ranged from twenty percent at Tokuyama to ninety percent at Oshima. However, it was not until 26th June that a fairly sustained bombing campaign was initiated. The job was assigned to the 315th Wing, whose B-29s had been equipped with the new AN/APQ-7 (Eagle) radar for high altitude precision strikes on specific targets. These planes had been shorn of much of their equipment, including all armament except the tail gun, to lighten them so they could carry heavier conventional bomb loads. On 26th June, thirty-three 'Eagle' bombers attacked the Utsube refinery at Yokkaichi to start the sustained effort. During the next seven weeks the Wing bombed the oil facilities of five Japanese companies and, in fifteen strikes, dropped more than 9,000 tons of bombs with good results. By the time the campaign ended,

A spectacular calling card delivered to Kagamigahara by B-29

Japan was incapable of providing fuel to support either its war industries or the shattered civilian economy.

Perhaps the most successful of the specialized B-29 operations was an extensive mine-laying campaign begun prior to the invasion of Okinawa. Initially, AAF officials had been opposed to diversion of the B-29s to this task, but were overruled by higher headquarters. The first mission was flown on 27th March and aimed at closing the western approaches of the narrow Shimonoseki strait to enemy traffic. Ninety-two B-29s dropped a mixture of 1,000 and 2,000 pound acoustic and magnetic mines into the strait. The sudden appearance of these mines surprised the Japanese and their initial reaction was to halt all ship movements until the channels could be cleared. The Japanese navy moved quickly to establish an extensive

B-29s head towards dramatic cumulus during the bombing run-up on Kobe on June 1945

system of mine watchers, stationed along the coast, on adjacent hills, and in numerous fishing boats anchored in narrow channels. Radar, searchlights, and underwater sound equipment also were employed to help spot the mines. But the Japanese found that they did not have sufficient mine sweeping equipment to handle the problem and, as additional mines were dropped, they had difficulty keeping the strait open.

Following a second mission on 30th March, LeMay ordered the 313th to drop a minimum of 2,000 mines during April. Early that month three small operations, involving nineteen B-29s, mined the approaches to Hiroshima, Kure, and Kure harbor. They immediately disrupted enemy traffic. On the 9th and 12th the Shimonoseki mine fields were replenished by new drops. By mid-April, after a total of 367 mines had been sown, the campaign was temporarily suspended while the Wing joined the attacks on the Kyushu airfields. Mining opera-

tions resumed on 3rd May, when eighty-eight bombers dropped more than 600 mines into Shimonoseki strait and the Inland Sea near Kobe and Osaka. Two days later the B-29s sowed additional mines to strengthen the blockade and also laid new mine fields at Tokuyama, Aki, Noda, Hiroshima, Kure, Nagoya, and Tokyo.

Japanese officials, as vital imports dwindled, became increasingly desperate and finally decided to let individual ship captains determine whether to run a blocked channel. Some vessels made it through, but others struck the mines and sank or were damaged and put out of commission. By 27th April eighteen ships of 39,917 tons had been sunk or permanently disabled in the Shimonoseki strait. In mid-May the mine laying campaign continued with 200 bombers unloading 1,300 additional mines into the strait and the ports of six western cities on the Sea of Japan: Miyazu, Maisura, Tsuruga, Fushiki, Nanao, and Niigata. These ports were closed from three to five days and traffic remained dangerous for many months afterwards. However, it was the Shimonoseki strait blockade which badly hurt the Japanese. The mines were soon tying up an average of eighty ships daily and, during May, they had the distinction of taking a heavier toll of Japanese shipping than American submarines. That month they sank or permanently disabled eighty-five Japanese ships of 213,000 tons, nine percent of the existing enemy merchant marine. Admiral Nimitz, quite impressed, congratulated General LeMay. In a message, he said: 'The planning, operational and technical operation of aircraft mining on a scale never before attained has accomplished phenomenal results . . .'

The B-29s continued to sow mines through June and July with increasing effectiveness. After V-J Day, the Strategic Bombing Survey listed a total of 8,900,000 tons of Japanese shipping sunk during the war and divided the credit according to the following percentages: submarines, 54·7; carrier-based planes, 16·3; Army Air Force planes, 10·2; mines (mostly dropped by the Superfortresses), 9·3; Navy and Marine land-based planes, 4·3; surface ship gunfire, less than one. The remainder, about 4 percent, was attributable to marine accidents. The B-29s, which entered the mine-laying business late in the war and operated for four and one-half months, had achieved a substantial success. In 1,500 sorties, they planted 12,953 mines in the heaviest aerial mining campaign ever undertaken. The Chief of the Japanese navy's mine sweeping section, Captain Kyuzo Tamura, later suggested that Japan's air forces could have been better used to prevent the sowing of the mines rather than trying to defend the cities 'because the life lines from the continent which furnished food and supplies were of first priority.'

Even while the successful mine operation proceeded, LeMay began a new, extensive incendiary campaign against fifty-eight smaller Japanese cities in the 100,000 to 200,000 population range. They started on 17th June with four low altitude night attacks on the cities of Kagoshima, Omuta, Hamamatsu, and Yokkaichi by 450 B-29s. This first mission set the pattern for future multiple city strikes, which continued until the war's end. On 19th June 582 bombers struck the towns of Toyohashi, Fukuoka, and Shizuoka and every third day thereafter four or five other small cities were hit with incendiaries. By this time, the Japanese people had come to dread the Superfortress more than any other American weapon. According to a Jesuit priest at a Tokyo university, the Reverend Bruno Bitter, 'it was the major air raids of the B-29 which psychologically affected the opinion among all classes of the population that the war was lost.'

Throughout this last phase of the war, the Japanese Air Force, in Arnold's words, 'assumed a condition of impotency.' The B-29s flew almost unchallenged, rarely encountering more than 'seventy or eighty planes. The situation was not what it seemed, since the Japanese high command had been carefully building up a hoard of 8,000 planes, most of them *Kamikazes,* for use against the Allied invasion fleet and troops trying to land on the home islands. The Japanese also had built more than 300 runways through-out the country, some of them simply one-way strips for the *Kamikazes,* ninety-five at secret sites in the interior. According to Rear Admiral Toshitane Takata, the high command believed that 'if we could destroy the invasion fleet when it came to actually land in Japan – although even then we could not win the war – we could hold out indefinitely for any number of years.'

With little or no air opposition, the Americans adopted an effective leaflet propaganda technique to undermine the Japanese people's support of the war. Systematic drops of leaflets on Japan had begun in mid-May, many of them being carried on regular

Trials were conducted by the B-29 with the British-designed 12,000lb bomb called 'Tall Boy'. Its size rendered necessary special modifications to the aircraft, and even so the enormous device had to be carried semi-externally

bomb runs. However, in July LeMay requested psychological warfare personnel to prepare a special leaflet to be dropped on several Japanese cities warning the inhabitants to evacuate those towns scheduled to be bombed. The first copies were run off on printing presses on Saipan and 60,000 were dropped on eleven cities during the night of 27th July by six B-29s. The following night the bombers hit the first six cities on the list with 3,700 tons of incendiaries. Warning leaflets were again dropped on 1st and 4th August, with attacks following both.

The Japanese who read these leaflets seemed to have been impressed. The manager of the largest plant in the city of Nagoaka told postwar interrogators: 'The leaflets had a great effect on the morale of the people. They figured if the enemy could announce a raid beforehand, the enemy was superior. When I read the leaflets telling that we were going to be bombed, I moved my essential machinery out of the factory. The removal . . . caused production to drop by one-third.' A Tokyo metropolitan government official remarked that, since the people found 'that Allied air raid warnings can be depended upon,' they began to believe all American propaganda and their desire to continue the war rapidly declined.

Enola Gay
and Bock's car

In July 1945 the new President of the United States, Harry S Truman, travelled to Potsdam to meet with Churchill and Stalin to discuss post-war European settlements and final plans for the defeat of Japan. On the night of 23rd July, at a dinner party attended by the Allied leaders and their diplomatic and military aides, Stalin announced for all to hear (including the waiters) that the Soviet Union would soon declare war on Japan and he proposed a toast to their 'next meeting in Tokyo.' General Arnold immediately interjected that, if the B-29s continued their current tempo of operations, there would be 'nothing left of Tokyo in which to have a meeting.' The next morning, the Combined Chiefs of Staff were provided some details of the Soviet plan by General of the Army A I Antonov. He informed them that Russian troops were being concentrated in the Far East and would begin operations 'in the last half of August.' This news was greeted with general satisfaction by the Americans and British, who had been trying for some time to get the Russians to tie up the Japanese army in Manchuria prior to the Allied invasion of Japan, set for 1st November 1945.

At Potsdam, however, a dramatic new factor had intruded a few days before. On the 16th the President received word that an atomic bomb had been successfully detonated in the New Mexico desert. After further details were forwarded to him, he consulted with his civilian and military advisers on what should be done with the new weapon. He also consulted with Churchill. They were unanimous in their opinion that it should be used. Faced with the prospect, in an invasion of the Home Islands, of huge casualties (General Marshall estimated the cost as perhaps 'as much as a million, on the

American side alone'), they determined to use all weapons in their inventory to bring about an early end to the war. Whereupon, to hasten the war's end, the President authorized the first atomic strikes on Japan.

The story of the Manhattan project which produced the bomb is a familar one. Not so well known is the related AAF project, which was organized to modify the Superfortress to carry the bomb and to form a special B-29 unit to conduct the mission. General Arnold was not informed about the atomic project until July 1943, when Brigadier-General Leslie R Groves – head of the Manhattan Engineer District – briefed him on the Air Force's role. Groves requested the AAF to provide a modified B-29 to carry the new bomb and conduct ballistic tests. Sworn to secrecy and, for a time, the only man in the Army Air Forces who knew about the bomb, Arnold was in a dilemma as to how to proceed. After consulting with Marshall, he received authority to brief a limited number of his people so they could take charge of the actual modification, which was to be done 'in such a manner that nobody would suspect the reason.'

Arnold took Major-General Echols, his chief assistant for air materiel, into his confidence and assigned him responsibility for modifying the B-29 to meet the specifications of the bomb, conducting ballistic tests, and organizing the combat element. In turn, Echols selected Colonel Roscoe C Wilson as his special project officer. The B-29 modification task was given top priority over all other AAF projects; Wilson was to refer all objections or challenges from any agency directly to Arnold. Wilson was subsequently briefed on the Manhattan project by General Groves, but it was not until October 1943 – after he was visited by Navy Captain William S Parsons, head of the Ordnance Division of the Los Alamos atomic laboratory, and Dr Norman Ramsay, a Columbia University physicist –

The Potsdam Conference which called on Japan to surrender or face 'prompt and utter destruction'

that he learned there would be two different bombs of differing dimensions. The B-29 would have to be modified to carry either weapon.

Wilson soon realized he would need help and he turned to Wright Field, where he had previously worked in the Engineering Division, and to Colonel Putt, long associated with B-29 development. Wilson explained to Putt the nature of the project and assigned him the task of doing the actual modification. On 1st December 1943 he also dispatched a letter to the commanding general at Wright Field advising that a B-29 would be provided 'for a project which is to be held in the greatest secrecy,' that Putt would be in charge of the modification, and that the work 'must be given precedence over any and all other development projects.' To preserve secrecy, several code words – 'Thin Man', Fat Man', and 'Silverplate' – were assigned to identify the bombs and the modification project. The explanation given to the curious was that the first words referred to Roosevelt, the second to Churchill, and the third to a Pullman car, which was to carry the President and Prime Minister on a secret tour of the United States. Some time later –

after Thin Man was redesigned at Los Alamos – it was given the new designation, 'Little Boy'.

In December, a B-29 was withdrawn from the 58th Bombardment Wing and flown to Wright Field for the modifications. The actual changes, which were limited entirely to the bomb bay area, were designed by Captain R L Roark, Colonel Putt's assistant. They involved incorporating into the bomber a new H-frame, hoist, sway braces, carrier assembly, antenna equipment, junction box, and a release unit and shackle assembly. As this work got under way, Wilson and Putt in late December 1943 drew up a plan to govern test drops of models of the bombs at Muroc, California. Two months later, the modified B-29 was flown to Muroc where the ballistic test began on 28th February with models of Little Boy and Fat Man. After the first twenty-four drops, the tests were discontinued while the B-29 suspension mechanism was improved and one of the bombs was redesigned.

The test drops resumed in June 1944 and were followed by other bomb design changes and modifications of the bomb bay equipment. When all the changes in the plane had been checked

Left: The B-29 'Enola Gay' that launched a new era in warfare by dropping the first atomic bomb to be used in earnest on Hiroshima. *Above:* Its pilot on that historic mission, Colonel Paul W Tibbetts

out, ın late August 1944 the AAF awarded a contract to an Omaha, Nebraska, firm to modify three additional B-29s, using the test plane as a model and following specifications provided by Wright Field. Subsequently, the order for modified B-29s was increased to fourteen, then to forty-eight, and finally to fifty-four. However, only forty-six were actually modified by war's end. Meanwhile, the Los Alamos scientists and engineers finally settled on the bombs' designs. Little Boy's dimensions were 28 inches in diameter, 120 inches long, and it weighed about 9,000 pounds. Fat Man was 60 inches in diameter, 128 inches long, and weighed in at 10,000 pounds.

During the summer of 1944 the AAF took steps to organize a special combat unit to deliver these bombs. From a list of officers provided him Arnold selected Colonel Paul W Tibbetts, Jr, to command the new organization. An outstanding pilot who flew twenty-five combat missions in B-17s in North Africa and Europe, Tibbetts had been flight testing B-29s in the United States for some fifteen months. Some of the key officers who joined him were members of his former

group, while others were chosen for their known competence in various specialties. However, Tibbetts was the only one informed on the nature of his mission, the other men being simply told they would be dropping a special kind of bomb. Soon after his selection, Tibbetts searched out an isolated base from which the special training could be conducted and finally chose Wendover in Utah, far from any settled community.

His combat element – the 393rd Bombardment Squadron, which had been undergoing B-29 training in Nebraska, moved to Wendover in September 1944 to form the nucleus of the 509th Composite Wing. The squadron was commanded by Major Charles W Sweeney. To make the 509th self-sufficient, it also was provided an engineer squadron, air materiel squadron, troop carrier squadron, and a military police company. The Group's final strength came to 225 officers and 1,542 enlisted men. Eight miles west of Wendover, Tibbetts had a bombing range constructed, which the group used for test drops of bomb models. Later, some drops were made at Salton Sea and at Inyokern, California, with models

151

containing high explosives. In all, the combat crews of the 509th before they deployed overseas in the spring and summer of 1945 visually dropped nearly one hundred bomb models from high altitude. Also, as in the case of all other B-29 units going overseas, the crews made the long flight to Batista Field, Cuba, where they practiced overwater navigation and simulated precision bombing.

While the 509th prepared itself to deliver the bomb, in Washington the first steps were taken to inform commanders in the Pacific about the Manhattan project. In February 1945 a Navy ordnance expert, Commander Frederick L Ashworth – who had been assigned to the 509th – was directed to carry a personal letter from Admiral King to Admiral Nimitz on Guam. It reported on the work which had been under way on the atomic bomb and on the probability that one would be ready for use by August. Ashworth also was made responsible for selecting a base site for the 509th. After he had delivered the letter, Ashworth discussed possible base locations with one of the Admiral's aides and with General Harman of the AAF. The latter strongly recommended Tinian as the base for the Group since its North Field, then under construction, was expected to be completed by June 1945. Ashworth visited the island, found the base suitable, and made arrangements to ˙have acreage set aside for construction of assembly buildings, laboratories, warehouses, and storage space for high explosives.

General LeMay did not learn about the bomb or existence of the special B-29 unit until some time in March, when Colonel Elmer E Kirkpatrick, an engineering officer, arrived in the Marianas to take charge of the Tinian construction. Kirkpatrick made an unannounced appearance at 21st Bomber Command headquarters and explained to LeMay's aides that he was on a mission of extreme importance and had highly classified information to give to the commanding general. He got his private audience and provided LeMay data on the project and his mission of building the 509th's special facilities. The B-29 commander had little to do at this time but to pledge his cooperation. Several weeks later, Arnold informed LeMay that the 509th would be under the 21st Bomber Command's control but that 'because of the experimental nature of the project, considerable control may be exercised from this Headquarters, especially in the initial phases, with regard to the targets for the primary weapons.'

As construction by Navy Seabees of the Tinian facilities moved forward, the 509th made preparations to deploy to the Pacific. In early May the ground echelon departed Wendover for the port of embarkation at Seattle. The men travelled by train in separate Pullman cars sealed off from the others for security. The echelon sailed from Seattle on 26th May. The air elements began deploying to the Pacific not long afterwards, in several stages, and by July 1945 the entire Group was in place. The aircrews immediately began practice missions using bombs similar to the real ones, but filled with high explosives. The remarkable proficiency they had achieved in hitting small targets from high altitudes was soon demonstrated. The bombers also flew a number of single plane missions simulating atomic strikes against targets in Japan, which confused both the enemy and other airmen on Tinian. The 509ths mysterious air – the presence of 'long-haired' civilians mingling with the Group's airmen – and hints of a unique mission led one dubious outsider to pen the following doggerel:

Into the air the secret rose
Where they're going, nobody knows.
Tomorrow they'll return again,
But we'll never know where
they've been.
Don't ask us about results or such,
Unless you want to get in Dutch.
But take it from one who knows
the score,

The 509th is winning the war.

While the combat crews were sharpening their bombing techniques in the Marianas, the atomic scientists and engineers during July 1945 were completing their preparations for the first test explosion atop a one-hundred foot steel tower in the New Mexico desert at a site known as Trinity. Two B-29s – equipped with a variety of instruments, cameras, electronic devices, and other equipment – were made available for the tests to record the fireball's intensity and other phenomena associated with an atomic explosion. Assigned to ride one of these airborne observation planes was Captain Parsons, who would also fly the first atomic strike. On the day of the test, 16th July, bad weather held up the takeoff of the B-29s from Kirtland Field. When they finally did get off, the pilots found it impossible to find the tower because of heavy clouds and thunderstorms.

The Superfortresses were still groping through the early morning darkness when the countdown reached the zero hour, 5.20.45am. After the tremendous explosion, General Groves later wrote in his report to Secretary Stimson, 'there was a lighting effect within a radius of twenty miles equal to several suns at mid-day; a huge ball of fire was formed which lasted for several seconds' which then 'mushroomed and rose to a height of over ten thousand feet before it dimmed.' The men in the B-29s saw the explosion from a distance. Groves advised Stimson that, while the B-29s were not as close as they would be in action, 'We still have no reason to anticipate the loss of our plane in an actual operation, although we cannot guarantee safety.'

After the President approved the use of the bomb, the Acting Chief of Staff in Washington, General Thomas T Handy, on 24th July forwarded to Stimson and General Marshall at Potsdam a proposed mission directive for the first atomic operation. They approved it and, the following morning, Handy dispatched it to General Carl Spaatz, newly named commander of US Strategic Air Forces in the Pacific. It read:

'1. The 509th Composite Group, 20th Air Force will deliver its first special bomb as soon as weather will permit visual bombing after 3rd August 1945 on one of the targets: Hiroshima, Kokura, Niigata, and Nagasaki. To carry military and civilian scientific personnel from the War Department to observe and record the effects of the explosion of the bomb, additional observing planes will stay several miles distant from the point of impact of the bomb.

2. Additional bombs will be delivered on the above targets as soon as made ready by the project staff. Further instructions will be issued concerning other than those listed above.

3. Dissemination of any and all information concerning the use of the weapon against Japan is reserved to the Secretary of War and the President of the United States. No communique on the subject or release of information will be issued by the commanders in the field without specific authority. Any news stories will be sent to the War Department for special clearance.

4. The foregoing directive is issued to you by direction and with the approval of the Secretary of War and the Chief of Staff, USA. It is desired that you personally deliver one copy of this directive to General MacArthur and one copy to Admiral Nimitz for their information.'

The next day, at Potsdam, at the close of the Allied conference, the United States, Britain, and China issued a Declaration calling upon the Japanese government to surrender and warning that the alternative would be Japan's 'prompt and utter destruction.' The Japanese answer came from Radio Tokyo, which quoted Premier Suzuki as informing a press conference on 28th July that Japan 'does not find any important value' in the Declaration and that 'there is no

The 'mushroom' over Nagasaki that marked the final blow of the Pacific War

other recourse but to ignore it and resolutely fight for the successful conclusion of the war.' Tokyo's rejection of the Allied ultimatum set in motion the first atomic attack.

Components of Little Boy, the uranium bomb, were brought to Tinian by ship and plane, the initial shipment arriving on 29th July and the last batch on 2nd August. That afternoon LeMay's staff prepared a

Twentieth Air Force field order to govern conduct of the operation, which was set for 6th August against the city of Hiroshima. The order listed two other cities, Kokura and Nagasaki, as alternate targets and stated that 'only visual bombing will be accomplished.' All other US aircraft were to stay fifty miles away from the three cities to avoid radiation contamination. On 4th August Tibbetts – who would fly the Hiroshima mission – took his B-29 up for a final test run high over Tinian. At 30,000 feet his bombardier, Major Thomas W Ferebee, toggled a 10,000-pound practice bomb and Tibbetts banked the plane sharply. Everything worked perfectly. At about this time, after consulting his crew, Tibbetts had a painter letter the name of his mother, Enola Gay, on the plane just below the pilot's window. On 5th August Tibbetts briefed six of his crews about the impending operation, but still refrained from using the word 'atomic.' His own crew was not informed about the power of the bomb until a few hours before takeoff, when he showed them photographs of the Trinity explosion.

Early in the morning of 6th August, at 1.45am, three B-29 weather planes took off and headed for the three target cities. Their reports would determine which one would be hit. Soon after the *Enola Gay* and two other B-29s taxied onto parallel runways and prepared to take off. The other two B-29s were observation aircraft carrying scientists with their recording equipment. Tibbetts revved up his engines and, at 2.45am, *Enola Gay* rolled down the runway, lifted off, and disappeared into the night sky. It carried an important passenger, Captain Parsons. Hours before the Navy weaponeer had consulted with Manhattan Project officials on Tinian and they had agreed that Little Boy should not be armed until the plane was airborne. This precaution was taken to avoid possibly blowing up the entire island of Tinian should the *Enola Gay* crash on takeoff, as some of the scientists had seen other B-29s do as they headed out on a mission. Parsons completed the arming task en route to Japan.

Before heading toward any target, Tibbetts waited for word from the weather planes, which cleared him for Hiroshima. The bomb drop was set for 9.15am. The *Enola Gay* arrived over the city on schedule, the bomb bay doors were opened, and exactly on time the bomb was toggled free. A parachute slowed the bomb, which dropped for about five miles. At the loss of the heavy load, the B-29 reared up. Tibbetts immediately made a sharp, 155 degree turn to get away from the expected shock, which moments later hit the *Enola Gay* as it banked, slapping the bomber 'like a tin roof.' The co-pilot, Captain Robert A Lewis, had been preparing a log of the mission for William L Laurence, correspondent of the *New York Times*. After he and the crew sighted the great fireball, he wrote: 'My God!' Within moments, the atomic blast killed approximately 78,000 people in Hiroshima and injured another 51,000. It completely destroyed some 48,000 buildings and half-demolished another 22,178. More than 176,000 people were made homeless.

The news of the success of the first atomic strike was relayed to President Truman aboard the cruiser, *Augusta*, then crossing the Atlantic on the return trip from the Potsdam conference. Pleased by the success, Truman personally announced the news to the ship's crew and then issued a lengthy statement to the press in which he described the power of the bomb and declared that, unless Japan accepted Allied terms, the United States was prepared to 'obliterate more rapidly and completely every productive enterprise the Japanese have above ground in any city. We shall destroy their docks, their factories, and their communications. Let there be no mistake; we shall completely destroy Japan's power to make war.'

News of the Hiroshima attack did not reach Tokyo until about the noon hour, but the information was fragmentary. A second report arrived some hours later but still the extent of the catastrophe remained unknown to the Japanese government. It was not until dawn, 7th August, that the vice Chief of the Army, Lieutenant-General Torashiro Kawabe, received word that the entire city had been wiped out by a single bomb. Broadcasts from the United States, quoting President Truman on the bomb, and millions of leaflets dropped over

Japan, brought additional confirmation. These leaflets, addressed to the Japanese people, read:

'America asks that you take immediate heed of what we say on this leaflet.

'We are in possession of the most destructive explosive ever devised by man. A single one of our newly developed atomic bombs is actually the equivalent in explosive power to what 2,000 of our giant B-29s can carry on a single mission. This awful fact is one for you to ponder and we solemnly assure you it is grimly accurate.

'We have just begun to use this weapon against your homeland. If you still have any doubt, make inquiry as to what happened to Hiroshima . . .

'You should take steps now to cease military resistance. Otherwise we shall resolutely employ this bomb and all our other superior weapons to promptly and forcefully end the war.'

Of these American statements, Toshikazu Kase of the Foreign Office later wrote: 'If a single bomb was equal in destructive power to the mass raid of a fleet of two thousand B-29s, with this lethal weapon the Allies could exterminate all life in Japan in less than a week.' It was apparent to him as well as other Japanese officials that 'continuation of the war was mass suicide.' The next day, 8th August, Foreign Minister Togo met with Emperor Hirohito and advised that Japan must quickly accept the Potsdam Declaration. The Emperor agreed and declared that the tragedy of Hiroshima must not be repeated. However, Premier Suzuki was unable to get the Supreme War Council to convene until the next day. While the Japanese procrastinated, the Americans prepared to launch the second atomic strike.

Fat Man, the plutonium bomb, and the only other atomic bomb the United States possessed at the time, had been assembled on Tinian on the morning of 7th August. On the 8th it was prepared for loading aboard a B-29 called 'Bock's Car', named after its commander, Captain Frederick C Bock, but which was to be flown by Major Sweeney. Flying with Sweeney would be Commander Ashworth, who was in charge of the bomb. That same day, 8th August, a Japanese investigating team – including Dr Yoshio Nishina, the country's foremost atomic authority – visited Hiroshima and swiftly confirmed the American claims. In Moscow that night, the Japanese ambassador visited the Soviet Foreign Ministry to get its answer to Tokyo's appeal for Russian intercession to end the war. An hour before midnight he was handed Moscow's stunning reply: a declaration of war. Hours before this news reached the Japanese government, Red Army troops were attacking all along the Manchurian border.

Events now speeded towards a climax. During the early morning hours of 9th August, Major Sweeney in Bock's Car took off for Japan accompanied by two other B-29s. After passing through minor turbulence, they headed for an assembly point above the island of Yakoshima, 380 miles south of Kyushu, which they reached at about 8.12am local time. B-29 weather planes sent out earlier reported to them that the skies over the primary target, Kokura, were clear and also that conditions were improving over Nagasaki, the secondary target. At about 8.40 am, Sweeney swung Bock's Car northward in the direction of Kokura. When it reached the city at the northern tip of Kyushu, the crew found the area partly cloudy; however, the bombardier, Captain Kermit K Beahan, indicated he could see enough landmarks to drop visually. Sweeney turned Bock's Car into the bomb run, its bomb bay doors open, but at the last moment Beahan's vision was obscured by a layer of smoke and the drop was terminated. Sweeney circled around to make a second, and then a third, bomb run but each time the bombardier was unable to see his aiming point. With his fuel running low, Sweeney had a critical decision to make. After consulting with Ashworth, he determined to try the alternate target, Nagasaki, some ninety-five miles to the south.

While Bock's Car headed straight for Nagasaki, in Tokyo the Supreme War Council convened belatedly to discuss steps to end the war. The Japanese leaders now had before them the additional news of the Soviet Army's march into Manchuria, an act they considered an outrage and violation of their neutrality pact with Moscow. Suzuki opened the meeting by declaring that the destruction of Hiroshima and Soviet intervention in the war made it impossible to continue the struggle. However, three members of the Council – Generals Anami and Umezu and Admiral Toyoda – argued that Japan should insist upon certain conditions before surrendering. Besides maintaining the prerogatives of the Emperor, they wanted Japanese forces overseas to be disarmed and demobilized by Japan itself, all war criminals be prosecuted by the Japanese government itself, and there be no Allied occupation of Japan.

While the Council wrangled, Bock's Car reached the outskirts of Nagasaki where, to Sweeney's chagrin, there was a seventy percent cloud cover and the aiming point was hidden from view. Faced with the possibility of an aborted mission, Sweeney proposed to Ashworth that they ignore their directive that the bomb must be dropped visually and unload by radar. The Navy commander consented and, a few minutes before the eleven o'clock hour, Bock's Car swung over the target, with the navigator and radar man in control. At the last moment, the clouds opened up and the bombardier shouted that he had the city in view. Control of the run was immediately returned to him and, a

The Articles of Surrender are formally signed aboard the USS Missouri

Above: One B-29-25 was completed with twin manned dorsal turrets, two twin-gun 'ball' turrets, and a barbette on each side of the nose. *Below:* The first YB-29 was fitted experimentally with liquid-cooled Allison V-3420-11 engines as the XB-39. *Bottom:* The third XB-29 prototype of the Superfortress – a forerunner of the many B-29s that carried the war to the heart of the Japanese homeland

minute past the hour, Fat Man was released. Seconds later Nagasaki was rocked by a huge atomic explosion which devastated the city and caused enormous casualties. An estimated 35,000 Japanese were killed in the blast and another 60,000 injured.

In Tokyo, Suzuki recessed the War Council and in the afternoon convened an emergency meeting of the full Japanese cabinet to again discuss the surrender question. However, the cabinet members – their minds benumbed by the cataclysmic events of the past days and weeks – were unable to come to any decision. The cabinet meeting dragged on through the afternoon and into the evening and not even the announcement of the news of the second atomic strike on Nagasaki stirred the members. About ten o'clock, Suzuki halted the session and hurried to the palace to report to the Emperor and to request him to call an imperial conference of the Supreme War Council. The Emperor agreed and also expressed his willingness to intervene if the Council remained deadlocked. A few minutes before midnight, 9th August, the Council members filed into the Emperor's bomb shelter below the palace grounds. For the next two hours they discussed and disagreed over what should be done. Finally, to the surprise of the participants, Premier Suzuki turned to the Emperor and solicited his 'imperial guidance,' an act unprecedented in modern Japanese history. In a brief statement, Emperor Hirohito announced that Japan must 'bear the unbearable' and that his decision was to accept the Allied proclamation. Suzuki thereupon stated that the Emperor's decision should be the decision of the Council and the meeting was adjourned. Several hours later messages were sent to the Allies through Switzerland and Sweden announcing acceptance of the Potsdam Declaration, with qualifications.

Neither those qualifications nor a threatened last-minute Army *coup d'état* in Tokyo prevented the formal surrender, which took place on 2nd September 1945 aboard the battleship *Missouri* before a large contingent of high ranking Allied officers. As the ceremonies got under way, 462 B-29s – representing every wing, group, and squadron of the Twentieth Air Force – roared over Tokyo Bay. In fifteen months of operations, they had suffered 3,015 casualties – dead, wounded, and missing – and had lost 414 bombers. 147 of the plane losses were attributed to enemy fighter attacks or flak or to a combination of both. The B-29 gunners, however, were credited with destroying 1,128 Japanese aircraft. In all, the B-29s flew 34,790 effective sorties during the war and dropped just under 170,000 tons of bombs on enemy targets.

There was an important postscript. On V-J Day, the Americans had on hand more than 3,700 B-29s but only a small number were retained in their postwar air force. Beginning in 1946 the bombers – assigned to the nuclear-armed Strategic Air Command – began periodic rotational tours of duty to Europe and the Far East. In the summer of 1948, after the Russians blockaded Berlin, two B-29 groups were deployed to England and one to Germany to back up Allied determination not to be driven from that city. Two years later, when the Soviet Union launched the Korean War, the B-29s returned to action, flying their first mission on 10th July 1950. Between that date and the end of the war in July 1953, they flew another 21,328 combat sorties and dropped 167,000 tons of bombs. Even as they participated in this latest combat, the B-29s were obsolescent. More powerful strategic bombers – such as the B-36 and the B-50 (the latter a modified version of the Superfortress) – had already entered the Air Force inventory. By the end of 1954, with the newer B-47 and B-52 jet aircraft making their appearance, the B-29s were clearly outmoded and were retired from service as bombardment aircraft.

Bibliography

Global Mission by H H Arnold (Hutchinson, London. Harper and Row, New York)

Scientists Against Time by James P Baxter (Massachusetts Institute of Technology Press, London and Cambridge, Massachusetts)

Years of Urgency 1938–1941; From the Diaries of Henry Morgenthau by John Martin Blum (Houghton and Mifflin, Boston)

Japan's Decision to Surrender by Robert J C Butow (Oxford University Press, London. Stanford University Press, California)

Way of a Fighter by Claire Lee Chennault (Putnam, New York)

The Superfortress is Born: The Story of the Boeing B-29 by Thomas Collison (Duell, Sloan and Pearce, New York)

Atomic Quest by Arthur H Compton (Oxford University Press, London and New York)

The Fall of Japan by William Craig (Weidenfeld and Nicholson, London. Dial Press, New York)

The Army Air Forces in World War II volume V by W F Craven and J L Cate (University of Chicago Press, London and Chicago)

The First Battle of Britain by Raymond H Fredette (Cassell, London. Holt, Rinehart and Winston, New York)

History of the United States Air Force 1907–1957 edited by Alfred Goldberg (Van Nostrand, New York)

Kogun: The Japanese Army in the Pacific War by S Hayashi and A D Coox (US Marine Corps, Quantico, Virginia)

Kamikaze by Y Kuwahara and G T Allred (Ballantine Books, New York)

No High Ground: The Story of the Atomic Bomb in World War II by Fletcher Knebel and Charles W Bailey (Harper and Row, New York)

Mission with LeMay: My Story by Curtis E LeMay and McKinlay Kantor (Doubleday, New York)

A Military History of Modern China 1924–1949 by F F Liu (Oxford University Press, London. Princeton University Press, Princeton)

Dawn over Zero: The Story of the Atomic Bomb by W L Laurence (Knopf, New York)

Hirohito: Emperor of Japan by L Mosley (Weidenfeld and Nicholson, London. Prentice Hall, Englewood Cliffs, New Jersey)

Samurai S Sakai, Martin Caidin and F Saito (Ballantine Books, New York)